THE WHISKEY REBELLION AND THE REBIRTH OF RYE

A Pittsburgh Story

Mark Meyer and Meredith Grelli

First edition 2017

ISBN: 978-0-9989041-6-0

Belt Publishing
1667 E. 40th Street #1G1
Cleveland, Ohio 44120
www.beltmag.com

Book design by Meredith Pangrace

Cover and interior process illustrations
by John Tarasi and Jessica Pierson Turner

LESLIE PRZYBYLEK
SENIOR CURATOR, SENATOR JOHN HEINZ HISTORY CENTER

"Who on earth is crazy enough to open a craft distillery in the Strip District?"

That was my first thought when I ran across stories announcing Wigle Whiskey's plans for a building across from the old Otto Milk warehouse in Pittsburgh in 2012. I didn't even live here at the time. Like so many other Rust Belt children, I grew up in the region and enjoyed untold summer misadventures in Pittsburgh's South Hills during years when the city hit its lowest ebb. (Not that I recognized that as a kid. There were too many other things to do.) Then I left western Pennsylvania in the mid-1990s, building a career as a history curator elsewhere. Sixteen years later, I was contemplating a return.

In the intervening years, Pittsburgh had changed. For me, the stories about Wigle Whiskey symbolized the transformation of a blue-collar "beer and burger" town into something not quite finished, but definitely new, a more adventurous urban community. A place still trying to negotiate its relationship between what had been and what could be. In that context, a group of dreamers setting out to resurrect the heritage of

Monongahela rye whiskey in one of my favorite parts of the city didn't seem like such a wacky idea. Hey, why not try it? Pittsburgh has always been a place where people tested crazy ideas. Try and run a steamboat all the way down to New Orleans? Crazy. Create a giant metal wheel more than twenty stories high that people could ride in at the 1893 World's Fair? Crazy. Manufacture a pull-tab to make it easier to open your beer can? Crazy. (But oh-so fitting for the 'Burgh.)

As it turned out, I did return to Pittsburgh, taking a job with the Senator John Heinz History Center. And one of the first places I visited when I came back was Wigle Whiskey. At the very least, it was the neighborly thing to do, since both organizations reside in the Strip District. Since that time, I've had the pleasure of working with Meredith Grelli and the crew at Wigle on multiple programs and research projects. Their growth and success over the last few years has been nothing short of astonishing. And yet, as Meredith and Mark argue in this book, in some ways what they're offering isn't so completely new after all. Craft distillers such as Wigle represent the rebirth of a once robust local heritage; a tradition that was lost, and one that is still in the process of being recovered.

Wigle's role in that rebirth has been twofold. While they were not the first craft distiller in the region, they were the first to bring whiskey back to the city of Pittsburgh. And just as crucially, Wigle's strategic decision to tap into the history and lore of the Whiskey Rebellion as part of their origin story added an aura to their efforts that gave it a different kind of urgency. Indeed, the family's active involvement with the political campaigning necessary to change the state's antiquated liquor laws animated the sense of "rebellion" with which they identified. This same rebellious sense fit well with the climate of the region: a "Whiskey Rebellion II" campaign in 2008 was launched to protest an Allegheny County drink tax. In 2010, nearby Washington County inaugurated the first Whiskey Rebellion Festival, a community celebration that is now one of the biggest draws of the calendar year. For Wigle, reclaiming this history gives the distillery a sense of place and heritage that goes beyond marketing and touches something intangible, yet vital.

It should be acknowledged that the Whiskey Rebellion as a historic event—the first major test of the fledgling American government—was never forgotten in western Pennsylvania. Multiple museums and historic sites in the region interpret the story; some have been doing so with nearly all-volunteer staffs for decades. Volumes have been written on it. Early accounts were saturated in partisan politics while new scholars began taking a more balanced approach by the 1980s. But increasingly today for many people, history solely accounted on the page or even at a historic site seems distant, abstract. History in a glass? Well, that's another story. It's worth considering. Savoring. Maybe more than once. If this volume, part of Belt's "Notches" series of extended essays that illuminate stories impacting the shape and nature of the Rust Belt region, encourages more people to sample both rye whiskey and the history of its rise and fall in western Pennsylvania, then so much the better.

This book also offers readers a unique perspective of the sense of mission and heritage that animates Wigle's team, the sort of drive echoed by other family initiatives in other Rust Belt cities that are seeking to add new vitality to neighborhoods and communities in the twenty-first century. It's not just about the Whiskey Rebellion, or the later role of the Overholt Distillery. This is history as told by industry insiders with the zeal of the convert. How could it not be so? To invest the time, money, effort, and emotion into something that even Meredith herself admits was "a terribly stupid idea," they had to believe. Throughout this book, recurring themes tie the chapters together in ways that speak to human motivations far beyond the mechanics of distillation, although some may argue that is motivation enough: the catalyzing force of family; the drive of industry and achievement; the impact of perseverance and vision; the intertwined paths of capital and resources; the age-old combustible mix of liquor and politics.

It's a story worth telling, one that encompasses events that shaped this region long before the industries that gave rise to the Rust Belt ever had a chance to collapse. A story that illustrates the emergence of new businesses that are again shaping a sense of place for this city that has seen so much reinvention before. So pour yourself a glass of Monongahela rye or mix up a cocktail from the recipes outlined in the back of this book, and then sit back and explore *The Whiskey Rebellion and the Rebirth of Rye: A Pittsburgh Story*. Enjoy this tour of the Rust Belt region's spirited past.

INTRODUCTION

Opening a whiskey distillery was a lark for our family, an idea inspired by a bout of wine drinking while visiting family ice vineyards on a trip to Canada. We are not a family of barflies. We are a family that loves great food and drink, history, and our region of western Pennsylvania. These are the things that brought us to rye whiskey. When we started our distillery, these passions fueled us through the first five years of immense financial investment, government lobbying, nonexistent or limited salaries, and persistent twelve- to eighteen-hour workdays.

In many ways, opening a grain-to-bottle whiskey distillery is a really stupid idea. The business of whiskey is a backwards one. The vast majority of what we produce sits in barrels for years and the traditional metrics of success—a break-even point, profitability—are quaint, abstract notions. But the very peculiar, long-term nature of whiskey distilling has freed us to approach what we do through the lens of a life project rather than as a traditional business. And so we've come to think of our Pittsburgh distillery as our love letter to the region and to American whiskey.

Our motivation to write this book comes from a similar place. America is currently undergoing an explosive rediscovery of rye whiskey; according to the Distilled Spirits Council of the United States, sales of the spirit grew 536 percent between 2009 and 2014. Despite rye's status as America's original whiskey, much of its history remains submerged beneath decades of marketing around the more popular Kentucky bourbon. This book is our effort to revisit that story, pique our country's interest in America's original whiskey, and revisit the remarkable national history that revolves around its production.

In the first part of this book you will read about the Whiskey Rebellion that pitted George Washington and Alexander Hamilton against rural Pittsburgh distillers, about how rye whiskey produced one of America's robber barons, and about how it helped give birth to the American steel industry. Much of this history is based in western Pennsylvania, as rye whiskey was to that region what bourbon is now to Kentucky. We do not attempt herein a comprehensive history of rye distilleries across the state, nor do we even approach Maryland's rye history, which is quite interesting and important as well.

While the area around Pittsburgh is now well beyond its industrial heyday, the city's name still conjures images of belching smokestacks. The rye whiskey that fueled these industries, however, has been largely forgotten in the American imagination—a history wiped out by the long slog of Prohibition. But the impact rye whiskey had on our country's first 150 years cannot be overstated. The western Pennsylvania distilleries inspired the country's first tax, launched the first test of federal power, fueled the businesses of America's great industrialists, and lubricated the Republican political machine. They're too important a piece of our national story to collectively forget. This short book is our modest contribution to this effort and draws on the work of many writers before us. Our hope is that it inspires others to capture the stories of the multitude of important distilleries that made Pennsylvania their home pre-Prohibition.

The second part of the book explores the current state of the American rye whiskey industry and where it may be headed. American whiskey never fully recovered from the dramatic blow delivered by Prohibition. In chapters three and four, we explore the consolidation of the rye whiskey industry—one of the most dramatic industrial consolidations imaginable in America—wherein we moved from tens of thousands of distilleries in the United States to just two major producers of rye. We also explore how this industrial consolidation resulted in one of the most stagnant and misleading consumer product landscapes in the country, and how the rise of grain-to-bottle craft distillers promises to reinject American rye whiskey with its original spirit of place and regionality. Today's craft distillers are channeling the fighting spirit of the eighteenth-century whiskey rebels. They're also situating themselves in communities much in the same way that distillers did before Prohibition—as community builders with a product intended for men and women of all stripes.

Rye is not an easy whiskey. It's big, spicy, and robust. At its most aggressive it can kick you in the face. At its best it has a character and depth singular to its grain. Rye has a backbone that made it the muse for America's classic cocktails—the Manhattan, the Old Fashioned, and the Sazerac—as well as the ones developed by western Pennsylvania bartenders that you will find in this book. We encourage you to sit back and enjoy one of these classic drinks as you rediscover the story of this lost American whiskey.

CHAPTER 1

THE WHISKEY REBELLION

On September 6, 1791, about twenty whiskey rebels, armed and in disguise, waited in the isolated woods near Pigeon Creek, thirty miles south of Pittsburgh. When Robert Johnson, tax collector for the US Treasury Department for the Fourth Survey of Pennsylvania, appeared on the trail, they surrounded him. They shaved his head, covered him in tar and feathers, took his horse, and left him in the woods. The heavy scent of whiskey lingered in the air.

Johnson recognized two of his attackers and soon pressed the sheriff for warrants. The sheriff hired John Connor, a cattle drover, to serve the papers. When the rebels learned Connor had been hired, they intercepted him. They tarred and feathered him, too, then tied him to a tree.

When word reached Philadelphia, then the nation's capital, George Washington, in the third year of his first presidential term, and his thirty-six-year-old treasury secretary, Alexander Hamilton, knew they had problems in western Pennsylvania. But the true depth of those problems was just starting to become clear.

Whiskey, Politics, and Hardship on the Frontier

The local whiskey rebels who attacked Johnson and Connor were largely Scotch-Irish, people who had come to America with their love of whiskey and knowledge of whiskey making. Back home, their grain of choice had been barley, but in western Pennsylvania, they had discovered that rye grain, grown in the winter and harvested in the summer for hay or straw, could also be distilled into a spicy, flavorful whiskey. It didn't take long for rye whiskey to become a way of life on the frontier. It was the "common drink"—consumed at weddings, funerals, and political debates. Men used it as a midday "strengthener" in the fields. Women drank it and gave it to their children for medicinal purposes.

In Washington County, Pennsylvania, in 1790, there was approximately one whiskey still for every ten families. And if a family didn't have a still, they formed relationships with neighbors who could transform their rye grain into alcohol. Millers ground the grain into a grist, and then cooked it at a high temperature with water. As it cooled, malted barley was added to the mash, converting the starch into sugar. A whiskey maker would add yeast to the sugar mash, and it would ferment into a low-alcohol beer, or wash. Then, a distiller would work his magic by turning the beer into a clear whiskey that was as good as cash in the western country.

It was good as cash because whiskey was widely bartered in western Pennsylvania. Selling it was also good business.

A horse could pull about four bushels of rye, but that same horse could pull the equivalent of twenty-four bushels if it were converted into whiskey. Barrels of whiskey were also far easier to transport over the mountains to the east than grain was. It also sold for twice as much out East, and that brought a lot of money back over the mountains.

At this time, Pittsburgh was a village of 376 people where wealth was concentrated among a small number of families. John Neville, a brigadier general with Washington during the American Revolution and the richest man on the frontier, lived in a mansion on Bower Hill, just south of Pittsburgh. He was one of the largest whiskey distillers in the western country, having secured a contract with the US Army, which included the drink as part of its daily rations. Neville owned a ten-thousand-acre plantation and lived in a style that contrasted starkly with the rest of the frontier. While most settlers made do with log cabins, Neville's home had expensive art hanging from plaster walls. Although many Quaker abolitionists lived in Pennsylvania, Neville had enslaved people who worked his land and lived in outbuildings on his property. His son, Presley, had been an aide to the Marquis de Lafayette during the American Revolution and served as chief burgess (mayor) of Pittsburgh. His daughter, Amelia, was married to Isaac Craig, an entrepreneur and quartermaster for the army garrison in Pittsburgh, who also eventually served a term as the town's chief burgess.

The Neville-Craig families dominated Pittsburgh society, politics, and power. They were also dedicated Federalists, fiercely loyal to Washington and Hamilton. And as the local whiskey rebels mounted their insurrection against the federal government, the "Neville Connection" became one of their chief antagonists.

For most settlers on the western Pennsylvania frontier, life was hard. They were hemmed in by geography and enemies: the British ruled the world to the north, the Spanish controlled the Mississippi River to the south, and the American Indian tribes, fighting for survival, were creating havoc to the west. With the Mississippi cut off, the westerners were forced to trade across the mountains to the east, which was an expensive, time-consuming challenge. Their pleas to open the Ohio and Mississippi Rivers for southern trade, however, had been met with indifference from the political power brokers in Philadelphia and New York.

The westerners were deeply frustrated with Philadelphia's inability to suppress the American Indian insurgency, but Washington and Hamilton had their own, more pressing problems. The United States owed millions of dollars to bondholders and foreign governments for their aid during the American Revolution. Hamilton also had to decide whether the federal government would assume the debts individual states had accrued by issuing their own bonds during the war. He likewise had to establish a system to fund the government and pay for the cost of the ongoing war against the native tribes.

Hamilton had struggled over the method for funding the assumption of debt, as well as for financing the ongoing cost of the new, federal government. The country had tariffs on imported goods, but no national domestic taxation system. An income tax was considered too radical. Some in the West favored a property tax, but many political players opposed it. Some in the religious community favored a "sin tax" on alcohol, and Hamilton was taken with this idea. He estimated that such a tax would generate an annual revenue of $270,000, which, when combined with the tariff on imported spirits, would cover the anticipated annual national debt burden shortfall. The tax would have the additional advantages of decreasing consumption and encouraging the "substitution of cyder (sic) and malt liquors." There were already state taxes on the books for alcohol, but such laws had never been enforced. Hamilton wanted to grab that revenue source before the states started to focus on it.

On January 27, 1791, Congress passed a tax on the domestic production of whiskey, the first internal excise tax in United States history.

Whiskey Rebels Resist

The new tax allowed distillers to pay for the actual amounts of whiskey they produced, or to pay an amount based upon their still's annual production capacity. Those who paid based on production capacity effectively paid one-third less than the distillers who paid based on actual production. Likewise, because small, rural distillers only used their stills periodically, they effectively paid a higher tax rate than the big distillers who operated year round. And since the rate was based on the gallons produced and not on the sale price, the tax rate effectively doubled if the westerners couldn't get their whiskey to the higher-priced markets east of the Allegheny Mountains. This disparate treatment gave the big distilleries a significant economic advantage and fed into the small distillers' perception that Hamilton favored big money and eastern interests. Many saw the tax as an arrogant attack on the "common drink" of the frontier by easterners who did not understand daily life out west.

Some feelings about the tax ran deeper than money. Many frontiersmen were veterans of the American Revolution, which had ended just eight years earlier. To people around Pittsburgh, Philadelphia's indifference and the imposition of a tax that threatened a vital trade commodity looked a lot like the actions of the British monarchy that had triggered the war. The whiskey tax, in their eyes, was no different than the Stamp Act that had ignited the colonists' fury against King George. For many on America's western edge, Philadelphia seemed to have forgotten them and was more interested in promoting financial speculation and deal making on the eastern seaboard.

Washington and Hamilton saw things differently of course. Washington was worried about the country splintering and the mischief that Britain and Spain could potentially cause in the West. Hamilton viewed the tax as fully justified since it had been passed by elected representatives and was needed to fund the army and militia to help defeat the native tribes.

He also thought the tax would benefit the common good by encouraging more moderate alcohol consumption. Of all the targets available for taxation, he viewed alcohol as offering the best combination of political justification and revenue enhancement. Although he knew there would be opposition, Hamilton was convinced it was time for the federal government to establish its supremacy in the growing country.

So the stage was set: East versus West, city versus rural, a centralized government versus a local one, the common man versus the moneyed elite, big whiskey makers versus small whiskey makers.

As word of the new law filtered west, it did not take long for the westerners to send a message back. Around the time of the ambush attack on Robert Johnson, delegates from the surrounding counties met at the Sign of the Green Tree tavern in Pittsburgh, near the Monongahela River waterfront, one of the two rivers that joined together in Pittsburgh to form the Ohio. They excoriated the new tax for singling out rye and other grain, and for disproportionately penalizing the westerners and the poor. They lashed out at the concentration of so much wealth among so few men. They also protested that the tax infringed upon their liberty in the same way British taxes had done.

Needless to say, Hamilton was not pleased with the response. He viewed the delegates' list of grievances as an attack on the very existence of the federal government. Isaac Craig, part of the influential Neville Connection, warned that the broad scope of the delegates' petition made him wonder if the assembly leaders were "perhaps secretly hostile to the existing form of government." In response, Hamilton turned to John Neville, Craig's father-in-law, and offered him the job of inspector of the Fourth Survey. The position paid $450 per year plus 1 percent of all tax collected. Neville had originally opposed the whiskey tax as a member of the Pennsylvania legislature, but he had later come to support it because it gave him, like other large distillers, an economic advantage.

Neville didn't need the money, but in the end, to the dismay of his neighbors, he accepted Hamilton's offer. The people of Pittsburgh could not understand why a man like him, who had so much already, would take a position that would put him in direct opposition to his neighbors. The westerners figured he was either plain greedy or that he had been bribed. Whatever the reason, John Neville became the lightning rod that drew the ire and fire of the whiskey rebels.

In Washington County, no one would rent space to Neville for a tax office; eventually, William Faulkner, newly arrived in the area, offered him a space in his house. Neville announced in the *Pittsburgh Gazette* that he was open for business and that all stills needed to be registered at Faulkner's home. The *Gazette* ad didn't harvest any registrations, but it did attract a band of whiskey rebels who dressed up as Indians, broke into the house, and shot up every room. Faulkner was not at home during the ambush, but he later agreed, upon threat of tar and feathering, to discontinue renting to Neville.

In August of 1792, as Neville stepped up his attempts to collect the tax, the insurgents called a second meeting in Pittsburgh, chaired by Colonel John Canon, who had served as Washington's land agent out West and was one of the area's largest property owners. Hugh Henry Brackenridge, the lawyer who would later try to moderate passions as the insurgency heated up, did not attend, but Albert Gallatin, a political adversary of Hamilton (though generally a moderate) did. The meeting, however, was dominated by militants from the Mingo Creek Society.

The Mingo Creek Society was an extra-governmental organization that included a militia, an alternative court system that resolved disputes quickly and cheaply, and a political machine that greased the wheels on the frontier. It wielded great influence in the rough-edged world of western Pennsylvania, but the political establishment viewed it suspiciously. The Mingo Creek men pushed their agenda hard, and the resolutions they put forward from the second Pittsburgh assembly alarmed the power brokers in Philadelphia and New York.

The assembly declared that the tax on the "common drink of a nation" was "unjust in itself" and "oppressive upon the poor." The men instead wanted a system that progressively taxed wealth. They resolved to oppose the tax with "every other legal measure" and, hearkening back to the days of the Revolution, they established committees in the various counties to coordinate opposition to the tax. The resolutions were published throughout the western country, and they included warnings that anyone who supported the tax would be ostracized from the community.

Washington and Hamilton responded with their own proclamation that the federal government would use "every legal and necessary step" to collect the tax. In 1793, however, they had to turn their attention to more pressing matters. The French Revolution threatened the European monarchies and led to a worldwide conflict, pitting France against Britain, Spain, and the Netherlands. Washington and Hamilton feared that Spain and Britain would use the world war as an opportunity to advance and consolidate their positions in America. To make matters worse, the administration was also trying to contain a catastrophic yellow fever epidemic in Philadelphia.

Emboldened by the silence of a preoccupied federal administration, the whiskey rebels stepped up their resistance. Anonymous notes signed by "Tom the Tinker" appeared in the *Pittsburgh Gazette*, threatening reprisals against anyone who supported the law. The rebels also continued to attack tax collectors. Philip Wigle, a Revolutionary War veteran, was "one of the most active insurgents in the western counties." One day he found Benjamin Wells, the tax collector for Fayette County, investigating his father's mill and attacked him. Later, with other rebels, Wigle attacked Wells's house. Wells wasn't there, but the rebels told his wife that he had to resign as tax collector. Wells refused, so six men with blackened faces, kerchiefs over their noses and mouths, broke into his house again with guns raised, demanding his resignation and any documents related to his collection of taxes. Wells surrendered the documents, including the commission appointing him tax collector, although he later rescinded his resignation. Prompted by Neville, who wanted the federal government to intervene in the increasingly deteriorating situation on the frontier, he made three trips to Philadelphia to provide information to the administration about the incident. Washington was so incensed by the attack that he offered a $200 reward for each rebel involved.

In other parts of the frontier south of Pennsylvania, distillers were also not paying the tax. In these areas, the tax collectors had simply given up, and the western edges of North Carolina, Virginia, and Kentucky remained quiet. Those regions, however, did not have a General John Neville who kept scratching the sore of the body politic. Sitting in his Bower Hill mansion overlooking the folks below, he was determined the tax would be collected, come hell or high water.

Neville and his tax collectors became the targets for the increasing frustrations on the frontier over the federal government's failure to ease the hard edge of life in western Pennsylvania. In the summer of 1793, when the Washington County militia met to elect officers, they burned a straw effigy of Neville. Not long after, Neville and his family were personally attacked while returning to their mansion from Pittsburgh. And as 1793 turned to 1794, things were about to get even worse.

Insurrection

Alexander Hamilton decided it was time to act.

Notices were published that the federal government would take action against anyone not complying with the tax. On January 4, 1794, an announcement appeared in the

Pittsburgh Gazette under the name of Robert Johnson, the tax collector who had been tarred and feathered near Pigeon Creek:

PUBLIC NOTICE

WHEREAS, A NUMBER OF DISTILLERS HAVE ENTERED THEIR STILLS ACCORDING TO LAW, THOSE WHO ARE DISTILLERS OR DEALERS IN SPIRITS, WILL TAKE NOTICE, THAT SUITS WILL BE BROUGHT AND SEIZURES MADE AGAINST THOSE WHO DO NOT COMPLY THEREWITH.

Robert Johnson

Collector of Washington and Allegheny Counties.

In early 1794, the Mingo Creek Society compiled a remonstrance to the president and Congress. The Mingo Creek men complained that the federal government had not fulfilled its obligation to defend them from American Indian attacks and also had not opened the Mississippi River to navigation. Having failed in these core obligations, the government did not have the right, according to the protesters, to demand taxes from them. Needless to say, the remonstrances were not well received in Philadelphia. They only served to buttress the administration's belief that insurrection was brewing out West. The remonstrance was sent on to the Justice Department so it could monitor the activity of the insurgent organization.

Working from information supplied by Neville, Wells, and other tax collectors, Hamilton, Attorney General William Bradford, and United States Attorney William Rowe compiled a list of sixty westerners who had not complied with the new whiskey tax. They secured subpoenas that required the men to travel over the mountains to Philadelphia to appear in federal court in August. The subpoenas were a bluff; the federal court did not operate in August because it was too hot. Likewise, a new law had recently been passed, which allowed the men to appear in their local court. Hamilton and the Justice Department, however, decided to proceed under the old law; they planned to muscle the men into submission without any need to have a mass trial. David Lenox, a marshal for the federal court, was tasked with serving the subpoenas. On June 7, Neville published a notice in the *Pittsburgh Gazette* requiring all stills to be registered with the tax collectors by June 30. By June 20, Neville reported to Philadelphia that no stills had done so. The westerners had made their move and now it was the federal government's turn. With some trepidation, Lenox left Philadelphia on June 22 with the sixty subpoenas in his satchel.

He crossed the mountains and started serving subpoenas in the near western counties of Bedford and Fayette. Unknown to him, farther to the west, the rebels were shutting down numerous tax offices. Benjamin Wells's office in Westmoreland had been repeatedly attacked by rebels, including Wigle, which prevented Wells from ever collecting a penny of tax. Neville had also subleased a room at John Lynn's Canonsburg inn to serve as his

Washington County office, but rebels had come to the inn and demanded Lynn's surrender. Lynn, barricaded upstairs, finally came out when the rebels agreed not to harm him. When he appeared, the rebels cut his hair and tarred and feathered him, leaving him in the woods for the night, naked and tied to a tree.

Lenox rode into Pittsburgh in July, unaware that rebels in the far west were roaming the woods, looking for tax collectors. He had dinner in the village with Brackenridge, who assured him that the locals would respect his authority as a federal marshal. Brackenridge suggested, however, that it might be best if Neville did not accompany Lenox on his appointed rounds.

Lenox did not take Brackenridge's advice. He agreed to have Neville show him around the western Country. It was harvest time, a time of a "kind of Saturnalia, when liquor was freely drunk." Lenox quickly learned that things were going to be different for this round of subpoenas. The first four men he served "showed much contempt for the laws of the United States." Things would only get worse.

As Lenox and Neville moved into Mingo Creek territory, word passed along the frontier that they were in the area, serving legal papers on whiskey men. Men began to trail the two officials at a distance. Around noon, Neville and Lenox arrived at the farm of William Miller, who was supervising field hands helping with the harvest. Neville stayed on his horse as Lenox dismounted to read the subpoena to Miller, a war veteran who had voted for Neville in the past. Miller had sold his farm a few months before and intended to move to Kentucky. As he listened to the marshal, he became "mad with passion." He felt his "blood boil at seeing General Neville along to pilot the sheriff to my very door."

As the scene unfolded, rumors spread that Lenox and Neville were taking people back with them to Philadelphia. Lenox and Miller continued to argue, and at some point, Neville realized that armed men were approaching. He shouted at the marshal that they needed to leave quickly. They rode directly toward the approaching men who let them pass. Rifle fire rang out, and Lenox, no shrinking violet, turned to dress down the crowd, who yelled back in dialects that confused him. Neville knew it was best to leave, and they rode away quickly—Neville to his fortified mansion and Lenox back to Pittsburgh.

While the two men retreated to places of safety, word of the encounter reached the Mingo Creek militia. Confusion reigned, then discussion, and finally a plan of action—the Mingo Creek men would go to Neville's house, capture Lenox, secure the warrants, and bring him back to be tried by a Mingo Creek court. The men selected John Holcroft, the infamous "Tom the Tinker," to lead the "thirty-seven guns" to Bower Hill to confront Neville and the marshal, and bring Lenox back for some Mingo Creek justice.

The men arrived at the bottom of Bower Hill around dawn the next day. Neville had armed his enslaved people and fortified his house; he was waiting inside with his wife, granddaughter, and a friend of Mrs. Neville. When he saw the rebels, he demanded they identify themselves. The rebels, thinking Neville was Lenox, offered him safety if he would surrender. Neville spurned the offer and fired his rifle, hitting William Miller's nephew, Oliver. The Mingo Creek men fired back, eliciting a broadside from Neville's enslaved people. Several more rebels fell, and Holcroft decided the house was too well fortified for further battle. The rebels retreated down the hill to Couch's Fort to regroup.

Word spread quickly about the initial skirmish at Bower Hill, and by day's end, approximately seven hundred rebels had gathered at Couch's Fort to consider their next move. While the rebel force was gathering, Neville had requested that General Wilkins, brigadier general of the militia, call out the rest of the militia to fight the rebels. Wilkins consulted Brackenridge, who told him that only the governor could call out the militia. The two men then met with the local sheriff and judges to determine if a posse could be organized to defend the Neville homestead. The sheriff explained that any posse he could muster was already at Couch's Fort, ready to attack Bower Hill.

The rebels elected John McFarlane as their leader. McFarlane and his brother, Andrew, were Revolutionary War heroes and well respected on the frontier. At around 5:00 p.m. on July 16, the armed men followed McFarlane up Bower Hill and took positions less than one hundred yards from the Neville mansion. Neville wasn't in the house, but was instead hiding in a ravine where he could watch events unfold. Unknown to the rebels, Neville had also been able to secure the help of his son-in-law, Major James Kirkpatrick, who had come with ten soldiers from Fort Fayette in Pittsburgh to help defend the house. The rebels put on a show, marching to beating drums and taking time to assume their positions surrounding the house.

Once his forces were in place, McFarlane sent a party with a white flag up the hill to caucus with their adversaries. They wanted Neville to relinquish his commission as Hamilton's excise inspector. Earlier that day, Brackenridge had told Neville's son, Presley, that his father should agree to resign to "put by the storm for the present." This advice was not followed, however, and Major Kirkpatrick, who was in the house at the time, informed the rebels' negotiating party that Neville was not there and so could not agree to resign. After this, McFarlane sent the men back to the house a second time, again under a white flag, requesting the opportunity to search the house for Neville's papers. Kirkpatrick refused, and when the men came under a white flag for a third time, they requested that all women and children be evacuated so that the battle could commence. The women left the house and went down the hill to Presley Neville's home.

The rebels fired from about seventy yards away and the battle began. After fifteen minutes, McFarlane saw a white flag being waved from the house. Thinking this was a plea for a ceasefire, he stepped out into the open and ordered the rebels to stop firing. At that moment, he took a musket ball in the groin and died almost immediately. The rebels were beside themselves; many of them believed that Kirkpatrick had deliberately tricked McFarlane into coming out into the open. All discipline vanished and the rebels started to burn the estate's outer buildings, eventually making their way to the mansion itself.

Kirkpatrick saw that his situation was hopeless. His soldiers surrendered and the rebels let them go, but they took Kirkpatrick into custody. Some of the rebels wanted to kill him to avenge McFarlane's death, but David Hamilton, a justice of the peace, took him into custody and eventually allowed him to ride to Pittsburgh. There Kirkpatrick rejoined the Neville Connection, which was regrouping at the home of Isaac and Amelia Craig. As the rebels celebrated their victory with barrels of whiskey they had found on Neville's property, the most powerful families in the western country were huddled together, licking their wounds, trying to absorb the day's events. Lucky to be alive, they had to wonder what the next day would bring and if anyone could restrain the anger aimed point blank at them.

The Rebellion Culminates

The rebels had crossed the Rubicon by burning Neville's house and engaging the US Army in a pitched battle. When they met at Couch's Fort the next day, their attention turned to Lenox, the federal marshal. They needed to stop him from serving more subpoenas, but more importantly, they needed to retrieve the subpoenas he had served. The rebels were afraid that if these subpoenas arrived in Philadelphia, the government would begin seizing the westerners' land.

The day before, while Neville's house was burning, Lenox and Presley Neville had arrived on the scene. The rebels' rear guard had detained them, eventually releasing Lenox into Presley Neville's custody after he laid his hand on the dead body of James McFarlane and promised not to return the writs to Philadelphia or to further enforce the whiskey tax.

A committee of rebels sent David Hamilton and John Black, a Washington County rebel, to meet with Neville and Lenox to determine if the federal marshal would honor the agreement. Lenox denied having promised to relinquish the writs. Neville and Hamilton called in Brackenridge who, trying to find a way to finesse the problem, offered to give a written opinion on whether Philadelphia could sell the distillers' land based solely on the return of the writs. After spending the night researching and writing, he delivered an opinion that the writs only started the process. He also offered to go to Philadelphia to defend any man charged under the writs.

David Hamilton wasn't buying it. The rebels would have killed Lenox on the spot if they thought for a minute that he would return the writs to Philadelphia. He told Lenox that he could not vouch for his safety once the rebels learned of the marshal's position. Lenox saw the lay of the land and "while a violent storm of wind prevailed on the water," he and John Neville escaped on a boat down the Monongahela through western Virginia.

Prior to Neville's escape, David Hamilton had visited the Nevilles and requested their resignations. They obliged, but

Hamilton found the resignations arrogant and full of loopholes so he refused them. At the same time, rumors were spreading of armed men gathering near Pittsburgh, ready to burn the village and take Neville and Lenox into custody. Isaac Craig, in an effort to calm things, removed the sign on Neville's tax office to show that it was no longer conducting business, and Hamilton secured the resignation of Robert Johnson, who did not have the stomach for further confrontation with the rebels.

As things seemed ready to come apart at the seams, the whiskey boys called a meeting at the Mingo Creek meetinghouse to consider their next move. Hamilton sent a note to Brackenridge, asking him to attend in the hopes of moderating the rebels' more radical factions, but Brackenridge tore it up. If he attended the meeting, Philadelphia might lump him in with the rest of the rebels. However, Presley Neville, who had studied law under Brackenridge, also asked his mentor to come to the meeting. For Brackenridge, going or not going was a high-risk gambit. This was a dangerous game, and, if one played it badly, prison or death awaited, whether from the rebels or Philadelphia. Eventually, he decided to attend the meeting, but only if he could be accompanied by Pittsburgh residents who could later act as witnesses to his intentions and actions.

Brackenridge expected to meet a committee. What he found was a mass meeting of men, many of whom had attacked and burned Neville's house a few days before. If he had known the composition of the meeting, he most likely would have stayed in Pittsburgh.

Things started badly when Benjamin Parkinson, a Washington County rebel, read a letter from Presley Neville praising Major Kirkpatrick's defense of Bower Hill, informing the men that Lenox and John Neville had left the county, and telling the assembly that the destruction of Bower Hill would not harm the Nevilles since they had plenty of money and property beyond the rebels' reach. This letter did not go down well and riled up the men to a high lather.

Parkinson then posed the question of the day: Had the rebels been right or wrong? David Bradford, a wealthy lawyer who also served as Washington County's deputy attorney general, rose to speak. The rebels had told Bradford that he needed to pick sides or else he could suffer the same fate as Neville. Bradford was torn, but on this particular day he came out without hesitation on the side of the insurgents. Not only did he support the actions at Bower Hill, he demanded that all others present publicly declare their support for the rebels as well. Now the men turned to Brackenridge and the Pittsburgh contingent who, because of their ties to the Neville Connection, the men instinctively distrusted. The men were like sharks circling for more bait, and Brackenridge clearly understood he needed to lower the temperature in the room. The question was posed again: Had the rebels done the right thing?

Brackenridge told them yes and no. Morally, it was right. Legally, however, it was wrong—in fact, it was high treason, and the president would be compelled to call out the militia. But he would have problems raising sufficient forces. For this reason, if the rebels petitioned Washington, he would surely grant blanket amnesty to make all of this go away. Brackenridge suggested that this amnesty petition was the proper course of action. At the very least, he told the westerners, they had to wait to decide until they had a more representative body; they needed delegates from all the western counties comprising the Fourth Tax Survey. Brackenridge's speech got a mixed reception, but it quieted the men, who were not sure what to do next. Men started to gather in small groups and wander outside. After a while, the meeting reconvened with the decision that another meeting that included delegates from all four western counties would be held in three weeks at Parkinson's Ferry, on the left bank of the Monongahela.

David Bradford, however, having cast his fortunes with the militants, was not willing to let passions cool for three weeks. Hoping to find incriminating evidence against the Pittsburgh moderates, he concocted a scheme with the "Canonsburg Committee" to steal the Pittsburgh-to-Philadelphia mail. Bradford's cousin and John Mitchell, a simple, hard-drinking Washington County man, successfully intercepted the mail about ten miles from Greensburg. When Bradford and the "Canonsburg Committee" opened it, they found what they wanted—letters from the Neville Connection and Pittsburgh residents to eastern politicians that denounced the burning of Neville's house, Bradford's speech at Mingo Creek, and the rebels' anti-tax activities.

Bradford wasted no time. In an act of extraordinary boldness, he and six other men called for a mustering of the militia at its usual meeting place at Braddock's Field, just south of Pittsburgh. Because the Pennsylvania governor was the only person who could legally muster the militia, the men were in open defiance of the government.

Bradford offered the men the "opportunity of displaying" their "military talents." It was time, according to the call to arms, "that every citizen must express his sentiments not by his words, but by his actions." The action plan was ill-formed, but the general idea was that the militia would march to Pittsburgh, now being called the second Sodom, and take control of the garrison and the city. Pittsburgh was in a state of panic as it readied for the town to be sacked and burned. In the out-counties, people felt an increasing power and a certain giddiness at the prospect of taking down the haughty Neville Connection.

Moderates reached out to Bradford to try to negotiate a resolution that would save Pittsburgh. Bradford demanded that the village banish Presley Neville, Major Kirkpatrick, and Major Butler, who commanded Fort Fayette. In addition, he wanted the authors of the stolen letters banished. Finally, the people of Pittsburgh had to muster at Braddock's Field to show their solidarity with the rebels.

Pittsburgh held a highly charged town meeting. The second Sodom was in a precarious position. At most, the town could only muster 250 men to defend itself, and Fort Fayette only had forty soldiers and wasn't large enough to hold many of the townspeople. The townspeople decided that Kirkpatrick and the letter writers needed to go. They advised Presley Neville, who had entertained plans to go to Braddock's Field, that he would be first on the rebels' hit list, so he decided to hole up in his newly fortified house at the bottom of Bower Hill. Because Major Butler was commanding the fort, they could not very well banish him. The townspeople then formed a committee, with Brackenridge as the leader, to communicate with Bradford and the rebels. Finally, they decided to march to Braddock's Field to show their support and solidarity with the rebels.

When morning broke, the townspeople gathered to begin the march. Brackenridge's new committee was at the front and the militia brought up the rear. As they approached Braddock's Field, gunsmoke from the militiamen's target practice covered the field, creating an ominous feeling among the townsfolk. Other militiamen were also crossing the Monongahela, coming to the mustering area. By day's end, a total of seven thousand men answered Bradford's call to arms, and the Pittsburgh committee and militia mingled among the whiskey boys, anxious to see what the day would bring. "Major General" Bradford rode astride a great steed, dressed out in "full martial uniform, with plumes flowing in the air and sword drawn," giving orders as he passed. The whiskey boys were dressed in the uniforms they wore when fighting the Indian tribes—hunting shirts with handkerchiefs on their heads. It was an impressive array of force, and the Pittsburgh committee knew they needed to tread carefully.

The whiskey boys asked Brackenridge if they could take Fort Fayette. Brackenridge, playing his dangerous game of deflection and delay, predicted victory with losses of at least 1,000 dead and perhaps 500 wounded. Some hard-edged, savvy militants distrusted Brackenridge and the Pittsburgh contingent, but the day dragged on without formulating a decisive plan of action. The militia camped that night at Braddock's Field, and in the morning, Bradford called a meeting of the militia leaders. The rebels wanted Presley Neville out of the area. The Pittsburghers agreed, but negotiated an eight-day grace period. With that settled, it was agreed the men would march into Pittsburgh, but not attack the fort, or burn and ransack the town. It would be a show of force with some whiskey thrown in at the end.

Word of the plan reached Pittsburgh. Taverns were closed, but the townspeople set up food and whiskey to meet the men as they concluded their march. It was all a work in progress, and the slightest wrong move could set things ablaze. With Bradford leading, the whiskey boys lined up for two and a half miles behind him. They marched down along the Monongahela into Pittsburgh, where the townspeople formally greeted them. Brackenridge gave up four barrels of whiskey for the good of the order. The militants wanted to burn the houses of Major Kirkpatrick, the letter writers, and Presley Neville. They were deterred, however, partly from fear that they would set the entire town on fire.

Rebels did eventually cross the river and burn barns owned by Major Kirkpatrick. As it turned out, Kirkpatrick had not left town as he promised, but was hiding out in the fort. The townspeople were beside themselves that he was still around, and they gathered around the fort, hoping to capture him. Presley Neville appeared before them to argue for Kirkpatrick, but realized quickly that the committee was not in a good humor. He told them that Kirkpatrick had holed up in the fort because he thought he couldn't make it safely through town. The committee arranged for an escort, and Kirkpatrick was able to escape under cover of darkness and rain.

Benjamin Wells was not so lucky. A few days after the mustering at Braddock's Field, Wigle and a band of rebels forced him to resign and burned his house to the ground. Wells went to Philadelphia to give witness to what had happened. Tom the Tinker started to loom large on the frontier, discouraging any cooperation with the law. Liberty poles, recalling the American Revolution, started appearing everywhere, proclaiming opposition to the whiskey tax. And looming on the horizon was the mass meeting at Parkinson's Ferry where the four western counties would decide whether or not to wage civil war against Philadelphia.

Philadelphia Responds

Back in Philadelphia, Alexander Hamilton, feeling besieged on all fronts, was working himself to death, trying to keep the government funded and functioning. Tax collection in the West was an abysmal failure. He had listened to criticism and made practical changes to make the tax fairer, but what good had come of it? The reports from western Pennsylvania grew more dire by the day. Seven thousand men were ready to sack Pittsburgh. Elites like Brackenridge, Bradford, and Gallatin were goading the rabble into insurrection. It was anarchy, all anarchy. Hamilton, young and intense, had been pushing for military intervention for some time, but Washington moved more cautiously. He yearned for Mount Vernon, not more war. The lay of the land had now changed dramatically, however. It was time to show the country that Philadelphia was willing to use military might to enforce its will.

As always, there were complications. Washington needed to get an army across the mountains and back before winter; he couldn't support an army in Pittsburgh, and the last thing he wanted was another Valley Forge. He needed to act quickly, but the army had to be militia. Politically, he needed the cooperation of governors to muster the militia, and he knew that Pennsylvania Governor Thomas Mifflin, a Jeffersonian and a longtime adversary, was not going to call out the militia against his own citizens unless he was convinced that every other option had been exhausted. Additionally, the Militia Act of 1792 allowed the federal government to use militia only if a Supreme Court justice certified that a state of "insurrection" existed against the government. If Washington obtained the certification, however, he could act with impunity since Congress had recessed. To go to war, he and Hamilton decided they first needed to build popular support by ostensibly seeking peace.

On August 4, 1794, Washington obtained a certification from Supreme Court Justice James Wilson that a state of insurrection existed in western Pennsylvania. He now had the legal authority to call up the militia, but he still needed to build his political case. He promptly issued a proclamation and, after reviewing recent events, declared that "many persons in the... western parts of Pennsylvania" had committed acts of "treason." He decried the "combinations" that were "subversive" of the "just authority of government."

Not unexpectedly, Governor Mifflin and the Pennsylvania men resisted the call for the militia. Hamilton pushed for immediate military intervention and worked to dissipate the governor's resistance. Edmond Randolph, Washington's secretary of state, argued that a peace commission should be sent west to negotiate. Attorney General Bradford concurred, but only as a matter of political expediency; he expected the army to march west and forcefully crush the rebellion. Washington liked the compromise of a peace commission and appointed Bradford, Pennsylvania Supreme Court Justice Jasper Yeates, and Senator James Ross, as the federal commissioners. Two state commissioners were also appointed.

Hamilton was not content to let matters simmer, however. Writing under pseudonyms in the Philadelphia newspapers, he railed against the rebels, painting them as "anarchists" bent on destroying the government. He wasn't interested in finding a nuanced, diplomatic resolution to the western problem. It was time for the federal government to assert itself in the most formidable way possible.

On August 7, as Bradford and Yeates started their journey west, Henry Knox, the secretary of war, issued orders to muster 12,950 militiamen from four states. The farther west the commissioners went, the more bleak the situation seemed. They met John Neville and Lenox, who were still making their escape from Pittsburgh to Philadelphia. The two men advised the peace commissioners that the West was lost to the rebels. As the commissioners got even closer to Pittsburgh, they met up with the escaping Presley Neville, who reinforced the view that leaders, including Hugh Henry Brackenridge, were inciting the rebels to break with Philadelphia.

Before they had even arrived to talk with the rebels, Yeates and Bradford urged Philadelphia to bring troops west. On August 24, a top-secret Cabinet meeting was held in which, under Hamilton's forceful arguments, the federal government started to prepare for war in earnest. Hamilton told Governor Henry "Light-Horse Harry" Lee of Virginia to begin to secretly ready his troops. He demanded that war orders be post-dated until September 1 for "particular reasons." The peace commission had barely begun its mission, and war was already in the works.

While Philadelphia was working its way through the logistical and political spadework of building a war machine, 226 delegates met on August 14 to discuss the next step in the rebellion. Senator Ross, who lived in the West, was there, although he did not yet know he had been appointed as a federal peace commissioner. Brackenridge and Gallatin were there as well, looking for a way to stop the runaway train. David Bradford, having cast his fate wholeheartedly with the rebels, wanted as many people on board that train as possible. The meeting was on Bradford's home turf, and he thought the majority of the delegates came predisposed to his view.

Bradford showed Gallatin his proposed war resolution. Gallatin, wanting to put space between himself and the militants, flatly rejected the proposal. Brackenridge seemed more sympathetic, and the militants, though distrustful of Brackenridge's friendship with Presley Neville, wanted him on their side.

As resolutions came before the assembly, Brackenridge succeeded in having them referred to a committee composed of himself, Gallatin, Bradford, and Herman Husbands. That night, with the committee scheduled to meet in the morning, Brackenridge stayed at a local farmhouse with many of the people who had attended the assembly. "The whole cry was war," he later recalled. As he lay on the cabin floor, his head on a saddle, he knew that if war came, his life was over.

The next day, the committee labored over the resolutions. Gallatin directly attacked Bradford's approach; Brackenridge parried with humor and deflection; and Bradford sought language that would bind the westerners together in armed opposition to the federal government. In the end, the most important product of the committee's work was to establish a standing committee of sixty men that would represent the western country in its complaints with Philadelphia. The subject of war was finessed by giving the standing committee the power "in case of a sudden emergency to take such temporary measures as they may think necessary."

When things finally seemed like they were drawing to a close, word came that the peace commissioners were only a half day away and wanted to meet with the assembly. Brackenridge and Gallatin knew this was a disaster waiting to happen. Things were not helped when Washington's proclamation accusing the westerners of "treason" was read to the assembly. Senator Ross told Brackenridge he had to keep the meeting from happening. Brackenridge knew that the peace commission was his lifeline. If they came with authority for a blanket amnesty, there might be a way to save his life and keep the country from civil war. Brackenridge was also optimistic that he could strike a deal. He personally knew all three of the federal commissioners and Gallatin would support him. He went before the assembly and convinced them that meeting the commissioners would be a waste of everyone's time. It was better to send a small negotiating team that could report back. The men, tiring of the meeting, agreed to defer matters to a negotiating committee of twelve men, including Brackenridge, Albert Gallatin, and the radicals, James Marshall and David Bradford.

The peace commissioners went to Pittsburgh for the night, where a mob immediately raised a liberty pole in front of their inn, proclaiming their solidarity with the rebels' cause. This welcome did not improve the commissioners' view of the situation in the West.

Brackenridge visited Attorney General Bradford that night, and found Isaac Craig regaling him with stories of how Brackenridge and the rebels had banished him and others from Pittsburgh. He intervened, gave his version of events, and told Bradford that he was not an insurgent. The attorney general's response was not reassuring, however. Brackenridge spent a restless night, now seeing that Philadelphia might regard him as an insurgent, and wondering if he too should just throw his lot in with the rebels. With the help of the Spanish, the English, and the Indian tribes, they might be able to beat back Philadelphia.

By morning, though, Brackenridge was again focused on how to obtain a deal. The federal commissioners demanded that the negotiating committee and the standing committee pledge allegiance to the government, submit to the whiskey tax, and renounce any violence against the government. In addition, the commissioners wanted every person in western Pennsylvania to publicly sign a pledge of fealty to the federal government on September 14. If there were no civil unrest for one year, the government would grant blanket amnesty in return. Brackenridge had the deal he wanted; he now had to sell it to the standing committee and to the rest of the people in western Pennsylvania.

The standing committee met in Brownsville on August 28 to consider the commissioners' proposals. As the negotiating committee reported on the tentative settlement, angry murmurs rippled through the crowd once they realized the whiskey tax would not be repealed. Bradford, who had signed on to the deal, trashed the proposals, stoking the assembly's rising anger. The moderates, understanding that things were teetering on the brink, successfully persuaded the delegates to break for the day and return the next morning. The Washington County men gathered around Bradford to caucus on their next move. Brackenridge, not knowing what the night might bring, went across the river to a farmhouse, safely away from the mass of men.

The next morning, he huddled with the moderates. The night had not gone well. Bradford and his men had spent the night fanning the flames. Some urged violent confrontation with those who stood in the way of the rebellion. Many thought Brackenridge had been bribed by the government. No-nonsense Mingo Creek men showed up at the meeting. Civil war was in the air. The moderates decided that Gallatin, a committed anti-Federalist and friend of Thomas Jefferson, would speak first.

Gallatin argued his case with passion, point by point, trying to diffuse anger with reason. He distinguished the American Revolution from the present fight, reviewed the concessions Alexander Hamilton had made on the whiskey tax, presented a method forward to seek repeal, and highlighted the concessions the committee had wrangled from the commissioners.

If Gallatin, the financier, presented the lawyer's brief, Brackenridge, the lawyer, went to the heart of the matter. War or no war—that was the question. If the rebels persisted, it would be a civil war against the other fifteen states, led by none other than General George Washington. Although they might parry Philadelphia's initial thrusts, they could not withstand a prolonged campaign. Washington would bring all the military might he had to keep the country together, and he had proven that he was not easily deterred. In the end, the West would lose, and the rebels would pay for it with their lives and fortunes. He encouraged the men to accept the amnesty, keep the West together, and continue the diplomatic fight to repeal the whiskey tax. There was no other way. He ended by saying he had done what he could, but would no longer participate in the negotiations.

After ten hours of speeches, Bradford took the floor. "Still for war," he exclaimed. He told the men that they could "defeat the first army that attempts to cross the mountains." They would "seize their arms and baggage." As he beat the war drum, he talked of independence for the West. Finally, the speeches were done, and the time of decision had come.

The standing committee voted in secret, thirty-four to twenty-three, to accept the commissioners' offer. They certified a resolution stating that "it is in the interest of the people of this country to accede to the proposals made by the commissioners on the part of the United States."

The peace commissioners, however, were not satisfied. They knew there had been a "public advocacy" of "open rebellion" during the meeting. Moreover, "two-fifths" of the standing committee had rejected the "indulgence" offered by the government, preferring the "convulsions of a civil contest." The secret nature of the vote showed that government supporters feared reprisals by the militants.

The federal commissioners offered one final out: Each man in the four counties must "declare himself openly" and give "his assurances of submission." The commissioners warned the committee that the President had raised a militia of 15,000 men, including 1500 riflemen from Virginia. In short, it was time to put up or suffer the consequences.

The committee caved to the commissioners' demands. On September 11, 1794, every man over eighteen was required to appear in his township between the hours of noon and seven to publicly declare allegiance to the United States and sign a document agreeing to "submit to the laws of the United States." Further, he specifically had to agree neither to "directly nor indirectly, oppose… the acts for raising revenue on distilled spirits and stills." Finally, each man had to agree to support "civil authority."

Confusion and fear reigned as word of the fealty vote made its way along the frontier. Some thought signing it was an admission of guilt. Others were fearful of repercussions from militant neighbors. In some remote areas, word of the vote never arrived. Brackenridge spent the day riding the circuit, helping to calm tensions in Mingo Creek territory. He arrived back in Pittsburgh too late to vote by the deadline, but was able to pledge his loyalty the next day.

When the dust settled, 580 men voted to submit and 280 voted in opposition. Two weeks later, Isaac Craig wrote to John Neville, telling him that the "leaders of the insurrection were endeavoring by a new finesse to lull government" into the belief that the rebellion was suppressed. He assured Neville that the "general disposition" of the people was that "no excise man shall exist in this country." Respect for law would only return to the

West if the "weight of the Executive armament" were "felt in this country." The Neville Connection would not be denied, and on September 25, 1794, immediately after receiving the commissioners' report recommending military action, Washington ordered the troops to march while announcing to the world that the federal government's "overtures of forgiveness" had run their course and that western Pennsylvania remained in a state of insurrection.

As Washington prepared an army of 12,950 men, larger than the army he led when he defeated the British at Yorktown, there was another assembly at Parkinson's Ferry in Washington County. The assembly adopted a resolution proclaiming complete submission to the government and appointed William Findley, an anti-Federalist congressman, and David Redick, to plead with Washington not to send militia into western Pennsylvania.

The two men were able to secure an audience, but Washington, with Hamilton present, would not budge. The troops would march to obtain "unequivocal submission to the laws," protection of excise officers, and to extract certain "atonements" for illegal activity. The army would behave, Washington promised, but the government needed to "crush to atoms" and extinguish any "flame" of insurgency before it spread. Washington thought he had put the fear of God into the emissaries. Soon after the meeting, he instructed Hamilton to issue orders appointing General "Light-Horse Harry" Lee head of the army. Hamilton marched as the army's civilian head and Washington returned to Philadelphia.

The march over the mountains was punishing. "No expedition in the last War, not even Hannibal's passage over the Alps, could equal the almost insuperable hardships we suffered," wrote one soldier in his diary. Supplies for the soldiers could not keep up. Washington left written orders that pillaging the countryside would not be tolerated, but as food supplies dwindled, Hamilton issued orders allowing the army to "impress" civilian property found along the march. The legalized theft of the westerners' hard-earned winter stores exposed them to deprivation and possible death as they entered the harsh winter. Whiskey poles expressing solidarity with the whiskey boys sprang up along the army's route.

Word of the army's approach reached the frontier. Bradford took a canoe south and was hiding on a coal boat when local militia found him. A Washington County rifleman singlehandedly drove away the militia and Bradford made his way into Spanish country where he was welcomed by the authorities. About 2,000 men who had not signed the fealty oath escaped into the wilderness rather than face the army's wrath.

Brackenridge, after a long night of indecision, in which he considered hiring a hunter to retreat with him into Indian country, decided to stay in Pittsburgh and await his fate. With Hamilton, Neville, and the army bivouacked between the Monongahela and Youghiogheny Rivers, Brackenridge wrote out his version of events for Senator Ross. If he was to be assassinated, he preferred that it happen in the comfort of his home rather than in some godforsaken part of the Indian country. Gallatin was also high on the army's hit list, but he enjoyed some protections as a result of his recent election to Congress. Brackenridge enjoyed no such advantage, and General Neville, traveling with the army, made sure Hamilton and the army knew that Brackenridge was "the greatest scoundrel on God Almighty's earth."

The Nevilles returned to Pittsburgh, entering triumphantly, making their way to Presley Neville's townhouse, only one hundred yards from Brackenridge's. That night a squad of soldiers went to Brackenridge's house with assassination on their mind. The Nevilles heard the commotion and called off the soldiers, but Brackenridge felt no gratitude. He knew they were saving themselves from possible incrimination and saving him for a much more public humiliation and death.

Working from lists prepared by Hamilton, the United States attorney, and the Nevilles, the army coordinated a massive roundup of suspects on the night of November 13, 1794. Remembered as the "Terrible" or "Dreadful" Night, men, on little or no evidence, were taken at bayonet point from crying wives and screaming children. The soldiers marched the half-dressed men through the streets in the darkness, across creeks that reached to their waists, and imprisoned them in damp barns. In one case they commanded the prisoners to eat raw flesh. Federal Judge Richard Peters had traveled with the army to provide due process, but Hamilton, invoking exigent circumstances, had authorized the arrests without warrants.

In Mingo Creek, General Anthony "Blackbeard" White took forty men prisoner and held them without food or water for two days, culminating in a forced march so punishing that the soldiers ignored White's commands and allowed the most feeble prisoners to ride their mounts.

Awaiting his fate, Brackenridge slept in his clothes for two nights. Twenty years earlier, he had suffered a nervous breakdown, and now he feared his nerves were deserting him again. He did not think he could overcome the bias of a Philadelphia jury, and he worried that a trial would ruin him financially and emotionally. Finally, the subpoena came, ordering him to appear before Judge Peters to give testimony. When he presented himself, he was instructed to see Alexander Hamilton directly.

John Woods, Neville's lawyer, thought he had found the smoking gun in the case against Brackenridge. There was a mysterious letter from Brackenridge to Bradford requesting papers concerning the "business." The Nevilles and Woods believed this was the missing link showing that David Bradford and Brackenridge were coordinating the insurgency. Hamilton called in Senator Ross, who had continually told him that there had not been any correspondence or coordination between David Bradford, the militant leader, and Brackenridge. Hamilton asked Ross if the handwriting in the letter belonged to Brackenridge. Ross saw that the handwriting was clearly Brackenridge's, but then he noticed something that had escaped everyone else in the room. "It is the handwriting," said Ross, pausing for dramatic effect, "and there is only this small matter observable, that it is addressed to William Bradford, Attorney General of the United States." There was a cold silence in the room. Finally, Hamilton spoke: "Gentlemen, you are too fast; this will not do."

Now Hamilton sat face to face with the man he had been led to believe had tried to start a civil war. For two days he listened and probed as Brackenridge explained the events from his perspective. At one point, Brackenridge thought Hamilton was suggesting he would be given more leniency if he incriminated some of the principal players. On the second day, Hamilton told Brackenridge that he no longer was in "personal danger" from the government. Brackenridge was free to go upon signing the notes Hamilton had taken. Emotionally exhausted, he found it difficult to keep his hand steady as he signed the statement. When word got out that Brackenridge had talked himself out of prosecution, Neville pronounced him the "most artful fellow on God Almighty's earth."

Others were not so fortunate. Hamilton had made it clear to Judge Peters that a critical mass of men needed to be sent back to Philadelphia for legal proceedings. Of the more than one hundred men dragooned on the Terrible Night, twenty were marched to Philadelphia and assembled before the Black Horse Tavern on Christmas Day, 1794. By the time they arrived, they were so spent and frail that even Presley Neville expressed sympathy for their condition. Following General White's suggestion, white pieces of paper were placed in the rebels' hats so that the 20,000 Philadelphians who lined the parade route could identify and jeer them. The returning army and the rebels marched down Broad Street, and the president emerged from his house to acknowledge the army's great victory. Washington again was the military hero of the United States—he had won the first revolution and now he had crushed the rebels. The friends of order, the loose political alliance of federalists who in many ways resembled the British Tories Washington had spent years battling, had established the federal government's supremacy.

Of the twenty men marched to Philadelphia, twelve were tried for high treason. The first ten were acquitted because the evidence was nonexistent or there were insufficient corroborating witnesses. Pressure grew upon the United States attorney and judiciary to justify the invasion of the West. Supreme Court Justice William Patterson presided over the jury trials of Philip Wigle, who was in the dock for attacking Wells, and John Mitchell, who had stolen the mail that led to the muster at Braddock's Field.

Patterson, an ardent Federalist who had participated in the Constitutional Convention, made sure these indictments would end in convictions. He instructed the jury that the "current runs one way" regarding the incriminating evidence against Wigle. To ensure that they did not linger too long over the concept of reasonable doubt, he proclaimed that "there is not, unhappily, the slightest possibility of doubt" of Wigle's intent to overthrow the government. Wigle, a simple man of limited education, may have been surprised to know that George Washington and Alexander Hamilton feared he might overthrow the US government. Both he and Mitchell were convicted of treason and sentenced to hang by death.

Petitions and letters flowed to Washington to show mercy to Wigle and Mitchell, widely regarded as victims of government overreach. Gallatin, once a prime target of Hamilton, filed a petition signed by the jury members who had convicted Wigle. Washington, having made his point, eventually pardoned both men.

And the Beat Goes On

Fifteen hundred militiamen were left in western Pennsylvania to keep the peace. There were reports that the soldiers killed animals, raised havoc in the taverns, looted houses, and attacked civilians. Some civil suits were filed, but the westerners had learned their lesson and kept a low profile.

After serving his second term as president, George Washington retired to Mount Vernon. The lands he had previously accumulated in the West increased in value by 50 percent once the Whiskey Rebellion had been suppressed. He hired new land agents to handle his vast holdings—Senator James Ross and Presley Neville. Always cash strapped, he listened to the advice of one of his workers and turned his rye into white rye whiskey and became one of the country's largest distillers. His Maryland rye used less rye grain in the recipe, so was a bit lighter than Old

Monongahela, the standard-bearer of rye at the time. Presumably, he always paid his whiskey tax.

Alexander Hamilton resigned from the administration in the next year and returned to law practice. He died before his fiftieth birthday in a duel with Aaron Burr.

Hugh Henry Brackenridge represented westerners in civil suits against the occupying soldiers, and eventually accepted Neville's offer to help prosecute western distillers for failing to pay the whiskey tax. He became a Pennsylvania Supreme Court justice and spent time trying to clear his reputation as a whiskey rebel who had talked his way out of prosecution. He was reputed to be a hard drinker in his later years.

Albert Gallatin became Thomas Jefferson's secretary of the treasury. During his tenure, the whiskey tax was repealed. It was reinstated in 1861 and funded approximately 40 percent of the federal government until 1913, when the passage of the Sixteenth Amendment allowed for an income tax. Without that amendment, it is highly unlikely that Prohibition could have gained significant political traction, since it would have eliminated one of the primary sources of government revenue. Whiskey distillers still pay the tax today—$2.13 on each fifth of eighty-proof spirits produced.

David Bradford, the militant who had escaped into Spanish country down the Mississippi River, found refuge in the New Orleans area, where he became a plantation owner. He was pardoned by President Adams in 1799. He returned north once to sell his house, which still sits on Main Street in Washington, Pennsylvania.

General John Neville never rebuilt his mansion on Bower Hill. He moved to Montour Island on the Ohio River in Pittsburgh. The island was later renamed Neville Island and became home to industries including shipbuilding, steelmaking, and chemical production. The home General Neville gave to his son, Presley, remains as an historical landmark at the bottom of Bower Hill.

Philip Wigle lived in Westmoreland County for eight more years before moving to West Virginia, where he died a natural death. His estate papers do not list a whiskey still as part of his property. Today, Mr. Wigle's direct descendants have made the journey to visit Wigle Whiskey, the distillery named for a common man who, like many others, got caught up in frontier excitement and almost paid for it with his life.

Hamilton and Jefferson's clash over taxation and the proper role and scope of the federal government still drives our modern political debate. The current conflicts between America's rural areas and urban centers mirror the same distrust that existed when our Founding Fathers walked the woods of western Pennsylvania. Folks on the frontier then viewed the financial power centers of Philadelphia and New York with disdain and distrust, a suspicion that eventually hardened into armed conflict when the larger urban distillers lined up in support of the whiskey tax.

The Whiskey Rebellion was also very much about class differences. The rebels saw people like the Nevilles controlling the economy, and they were tired of their voices not being heard in Philadelphia or Washington. They responded in the only way they knew how. The concentration of wealth in the hands of a few elites was very much on their minds just as it is in the United States of the twenty-first century.

Seventy years after the rebellion, Abraham Lincoln could look back at Washington and Hamilton's uncompromising resolve to keep the country united and find the determination to outlast General "Light-Horse Harry" Lee's son, Robert E. Lee, in the Civil War. Lincoln dismissed those who complained that his general, Ulysses S. Grant, was too fond of whiskey, suggesting instead that if he knew which brand Grant favored, he would send the same to all of his other generals.

CHAPTER 2

A LOVE STORY

S even years after the federal government quelled the Whiskey Rebellion, the United States electorate chose Thomas Jefferson as its third president based on his very popular platform of eliminating the whiskey tax. The promise of a whiskey-bathed frontier continued to pull the adventurous and the hopeful westward across the Alleghenies toward Pittsburgh.

One of the families to heed this call was a group of Philadelphia Mennonite farmers, the Overholts. It's not clear exactly what motivated them to make the arduous trip west from Bucks County, Pennsylvania—perhaps it was the promise of fertile land, the booming whiskey industry, or the network of rivers in western Pennsylvania that could take products throughout the country and on to Europe.

Whatever the reason, according to K.R. Overholt Critchfield's edited account of her family's history, Henry and Anna Overholt packed up their family—thirty-two folks, including children, grandchildren, and in-laws—in a caravan of Conestoga wagons and set off across the state. They stopped in western Pennsylvania at Broad Ford, named by George

Washington when he had surveyed the land firsthand. It was here, in 1803, that the Overholts decided they would make a life. And so it was here that Henry's son, Abraham, grew into the father of American distilling over the next fifty years, creating Old Farm Pure Rye, the gold standard of American whiskey.

According to this same account, "Henry and his family built their homestead upon 150 acres and Henry thereupon stationed himself at the family loom, which was conveniently close to the family still."

Abraham's weaving and distilling responsibilities provided him with plenty of alone time. Perhaps more than the rest of his family, he had the time and quiet to think deeply about the whiskey he and his neighbors were producing. He recognized a ripe opportunity. America's young government had not taxed any other industry in this manner, and it certainly hadn't enlisted an army of 13,000 men to protect its stake in any other business.

Abraham, by several accounts, was known to be an exceptionally thoughtful man. The economics of whiskey, however, were clear to most farmers of the day. While grain sold for a few cents a bushel in the early 1800s, whiskey, which shipped more easily and was non-perishable, commanded a commendable dollar per gallon. Furthermore, Abraham and others in his community of German settlers spotted an opening in the market. The Scotch-Irish, the real trailblazers on the western frontier, were moving to Kentucky to get beyond the reach of federal tax collectors after the Whiskey Rebellion. This left land, infrastructure, and opportunity for the Germans who had come in their wake.

And so, in 1810, against the wishes of their local Mennonite Church, the Overholts began distilling rye whiskey in earnest. Initially distilling a modest three to four bushels of rye per day, the Overholts immediately expanded. By 1811, their farm housed two 150-gallon stills. In line with many other farms' still capacities, Abraham continued distilling in this manner, steadily building his whiskey's reputation until he inherited the farm in 1818. At this point, he increased the capacity of his operation in serial one-hundred-gallon spurts over the course of the next ten years.

As Abraham's whiskey production grew, so did its reputation. Old Farm Pure Rye migrated westward in wagon trains; riverboats carried it south down the Mississippi; wagons traveling to Lancaster distributed it eastward to Philadelphia and New York. Abraham's whiskey traveled as far west as California, where it became the reward for gold rushers after a day of digging. In the course of just four decades, Old Farm Pure Rye became the nation's signature whiskey.

At this time, folks were drinking their fair share of the spirits. Some of Overholt's customers consumed as much as one gallon of whiskey per month. And the distillery records show that during the summer, whiskey buying hit its peak, with customers purchasing it in four- to ten-gallon lots, presumably to make bounce—whiskey flavored with seasonal berries and other fruits.

Abraham, unsurprisingly, was doing quite well for himself and his family. Across from his first distillery, the Overholts built a mansion—a gracious, substantial brick building surrounded by acres of farmland. He also assembled a staff of fifteen men. By 1829, the Overholt Distillery was an impressive four-still operation.

Nine years later, Abraham overcame one of his greatest obstacles to increasing production—his reliance on the community mill. Up to this point, his sons had transported the grain by oxen to the community mill, a dreaded task that was usually completed in spite of broken wagon wheels and obstinate oxen. But these trips ended when Abraham built a stone gristmill on his farm. This represented a significant capital expansion for his distillery, and made it nearly self-sufficient. It also introduced a new staff position, that of a miller.

One of Abraham's least effective and most-gossiped-about workers was his assistant miller, John Frick. John was known as a romantic, a man who wanted to be an artist, but instead found himself toiling away at a gristmill. In polite circles, he was called unconventional, and in private, rowdy. To make matters worse for him, his bright red crop of hair announced his Irish roots, an unfortunate heritage at a time when German émigrés were the premier class.

Abraham had eight children, including a daughter named Elizabeth, who fell in love with John. Upon hearing of John and Elizabeth's trysts, the Overholts were not pleased. As Frick's great-granddaughter, Martha Frick Symington Sanger, writes in her beautiful biography of the family, when "Elizabeth Overholt...announced her engagement to John W. Frick, a locally born, red-haired towdy whose...paternal grandmother was a red-haired Irishwoman, Abraham was furious." Elizabeth remained resolute in her affection for John in spite of her family's disapproval, however. When she told them she was several months pregnant with John's child, Abraham and his wife begrudgingly hastened to see the two of them married.

In 1847, John and Elizabeth moved into a worker house together on the distillery grounds. The house was described as a "spring house," which had previously been used as a smokehouse and summer kitchen—the equivalent of converting a broom closet into an office today. The snug stone cottage sat quite literally in the shadow of the three-story Overholt mansion. After giving birth to a daughter, Elizabeth quickly became pregnant again. They named their second child, born December 19, 1849, in the shadow of the country's premier whiskey distillery, Henry Clay Frick.

Henry Clay grew up in a much different manner than his mother had. His father received $30 a month for his work at the Overholt Mill. This income represented his father's entire personal estate, which starkly contrasted the wealth of the Overholts. Abraham's estate was valued at $400,000 in 1870, and John Frick's brother-in-law owned real estate that alone was worth $137,000.

John Frick remained the black sheep of the Overholt family, never able to bridge the gap between his poor Irish background and his in-laws' wealth. Abraham, it seems, was not immediately fond of Henry Clay, either. In spite of this, the young boy grew up watching his grandfather closely. He did not begrudge his grandfather for holding him or his father at arm's length. Rather, he admired Abraham tremendously and identified with the prosperity of his mother's side of the family. Frick even adopted the stately attire of his grandparents—both distinguished Mennonite dressers who wore black silk and cashmere.

Like his father, Henry Clay was not a guy's guy. Called "Clay" by his friends and family, he was particular, well-dressed, and frail, poorly suited for production work in the distillery. His older sister and his grandmother, both named Maria, doted on him and did their best to keep him well. He made up for his physical shortcomings with his intelligence.

Fortunately, Henry Clay, who was enamored with business from an early age, was surrounded by industrial growth throughout his childhood and young adult life. It was after he was born that Abraham undertook his most concerted and successful phase of distillery growth. In 1850, not only did he have a mill to grind his farm's grain into grist for his whiskey, but he also introduced a malthouse on the distillery grounds to malt the grains prior to milling. Furthermore, he built a cooperage that produced an extraordinary twelve thousand casks of whiskey per year. In 1856, Abraham added a trail of pens, housing 249 hogs. He fattened them with stillage, the waste product of distillation, and sold them at market. Then in 1859, when Henry Clay was ten years old, Abraham built Broadford Distillery, a six-story structure for milling and distilling.

This was a heady era, not only for the Overholt Distillery, but also for western Pennsylvania rye as a class. By the early nineteenth century, Pittsburgh was making half a barrel of whiskey for every man, woman, and child in the country each year. The style of whiskey that the Overholt Distillery produced—Old Monongahela Rye—became the benchmark by which all other whiskeys were judged. According to the US Census, Western Pennsylvania boasted 1,010 licensed distilleries in 1840, but this number likely does not capture all the family stills that littered the agricultural landscape. That amounts to a licensed distillery for every twenty Pittsburgh residents. That same year, western Pennsylvania distilled 644,722 gallons of spirits, and nearly a third of that was produced in the county inhabited by the Overholt Distillery. In *Moby-Dick*, published in 1851, the *Pequod's* second mate, Stubb, in a celebratory mood after harpooning a whale, yearns for a glass of whiskey. He mentions three great whiskeys in the world, the last one being the "unspeakable Old Monongahela."

With each of Abraham's expansions, he improved the efficiency and integration of his distillery operation. With increased capacity, his distillery was able to produce an extraordinary 860 gallons of whiskey per day. By contrast, a large craft distillery today, even with its modern advantages, might produce one-tenth of Overholt's production.

As Abraham's operation grew, nearby Pittsburgh was experiencing its own industrial boom. An influx of German and Irish immigrants made their way to the region, home to approximately 122,000 people, to fill industrial jobs. While the rest of the country relied on charcoal for their energy, Pittsburgh began using cheaper and more efficient coal to heat homes and businesses. Pittsburgh, which burned more coal than any other American city, was dubbed the Smoky City.

Abraham first dug up coal on his land in 1820 while looking for a spring. It so happened that the coal that he dug from his West Overton land was part of the Pittsburgh seam, the richest coal seam in the entire United States. And the most abundant strip of this famous seam, the three miles packed with the deepest deposits and the greatest economic promise—the Connellsville Seam—surrounded his distilling operation. Abraham uncovered the famous Connellsville coal, but it was his grandson, Henry Clay, who ultimately seized the full breadth of its opportunity.

For a time, even with this abundance of coal at their feet, Abraham and his neighboring farmers in western Pennsylvania focused their production pursuits on whiskey because of its easy transport and hefty profits. The coal Abraham dug from his land was fuel to grow his distillery operation, but it was not mined as a product for sale itself.

However, with the Civil War, the market for coal became undeniable. During the war, the Pittsburgh region became an epicenter for arms production. Eyeing the tremendous increased need for fuel, the Overholts made a fortune buying and selling coal rights to their neighbors' land. During these years, the Northern troops came to rely on the Overholts for two essentials: Old Farm Pure Rye Whiskey, which became the unofficial whiskey of the Union troops and President Lincoln, and the coal beneath their land.

During the war, Henry Clay was a young teenager, working as an office boy in the Broadford Distillery for $25 per month. Economic success stories were emerging in the Pittsburgh community, including one of a young capitalist named Andrew Carnegie, who was reportedly earning an astonishing $50,000 per year. Henry Clay, surrounded by wealth and industry, had lofty financial goals and dreamt of being a millionaire by the time he was thirty. He knew that wouldn't happen if he remained an office boy.

So he decided to pack up and move to Pittsburgh to work as a salesman in upper-crust haberdasheries. He quickly developed a reputation as the most productive salesman everywhere he worked. He easily charmed the ladies who came in to shop, and was soon making more money than he had been at his family's distillery. In 1869, however, he contracted typhoid, which sent him home. Just as they had over the course of his childhood, his grandmother and sister nursed him back to health.

Abraham was duly impressed by the independence and ambition that his grandson demonstrated during his time in Pittsburgh. To test his talents further, Abraham appointed him chief bookkeeper of the Broadford Distillery in 1869 with an annual salary of $1,000—not quite in millionaire territory yet, but a nice bump from his office boy wage.

Henry Clay proved himself a talented manager of the distillery's accounts. He also began to flex his entrepreneurial muscle with his grandfather's guidance. He purchased 300 acres of his neighbors' land and established his first fifty coke ovens.

Abraham grew especially close to his grandson during these entrepreneurial years. So it was a devastating surprise to Henry Clay when his grandfather passed away in 1870 and left nothing of his large estate to him. The silver lining in the inheritance was that Frick gained a controlling interest in the Old Farm Pure Rye Distillery, which in 1870 earned $40,512 (in excess of $1 million today). The family renamed the whiskey Old Overholt in honor of Abraham.

Even with this healthy revenue stream, whiskey no longer seemed to offer the same financial promise to Frick that it once did. He had witnessed firsthand in Pittsburgh the economic power of coal, and he saw the weight of his family's fortune shifting to this alternative fuel. While he maintained his bookkeeping post at the Overholt Distillery, he purchased twenty acres of land nearby and became the manager of the mine without pay. Emboldened by what he came to know of the coal business, Frick began putting together packages of personal loans, backed by the famous Overholt Whiskey name, drawing on the community's trust of his family's legacy.

Frick was full of ambition, according to one anonymous account:

"In the evenings, after finishing with the accounts at the Distillery, [Frick] drove throughout the whole region, sometimes on horseback, sometimes in a buckboard calling upon farmers. He optioned coal land right and left. His savings were exhausted with the payment of hand money and he borrowed everywhere he could. He rushed about the whole night long, with sheaves of promissory notes in his coat pocket—optioning, optioning!"

With land in hand, Frick set out to build more coke ovens. He understood that the market would move from coal to coke, which was easier to transport and burned more efficiently. In Pittsburgh, Andrew Carnegie continued to grow his iron mills and was in desperate need of coke to fuel his enterprise. The coal coming out of the West Overton area was quickly becoming known as the best coal for making coke. Frick was anxious to get ahead of the market and meet Carnegie's needs.

One obstacle stood between Frick and his ovens: he was out of cash. He did, however, happen to own the famous Overholt Distillery. So at twenty-one years of age, he traveled into Pittsburgh to visit the bank of Judge Thomas Mellon, also formerly of Westmoreland County, and an old friend of his grandfather. Mellon also came from a farming and distilling family, and so his agreement to meet with the young Frick was likely a favor to his old friend, Abraham.

Using the Overholt Distillery as collateral, the very determined Henry Clay convinced Mellon to loan him $10,000. Just a couple of months later, he returned to Mellon's office to request another $10,000. Concerned that Frick had so quickly burned through his first loan, Mellon sent his partner out to examine Frick's operation and determine how all the funds were being spent. The examiner's report deemed Frick was too distracted by his distillery bookkeeping and his art, which seemed to be an interest inherited from his father. (Frick's proclivity for art collecting would manifest years later with two major collections—one in Pittsburgh and the other in New York City.) Mellon, however, viewed Frick's distillery salary as an asset rather than a risk, and sent another advisor for a second opinion, who filed a more positive report. Frick received a second $10,000 loan from Mellon to build another group of coke ovens, according to Mellon biographer David Koskoff.

By 1871, Frick boasted 1,200 coke ovens to his name, and in another year, his company became the largest single coke works in America. He built railroad tracks and bridges to ensure the transport of his products. No longer a pastoral landscape, Connellsville now contained railroads running eight to ten tracks thick. Frick was transforming the place his grandfather had settled, and the community around West Overton had begun its evolution from America's whiskey town into America's coal town.

Industrial growth seemed to have its full grip on West Overton and Connellsville, but in two years, everything turned quiet for a time. Eighteen seventy-three opened with fortitude. The construction of railroads and steel mills, which were financed through bonds sold in Europe, continued at a fast clip. However, a financial panic struck Europe by spring, which soon crippled the heavily-leveraged enterprises in western Pennsylvania. The price of coal and coke plummeted, forcing most suppliers to halt production. America's burgeoning workforce spiraled into a 25 percent unemployment rate.

Frick decided to soldier onwards, betting that the economy would ultimately pick back up. The steel industry did of course bounce back, and with ferocity. Frick was able to increase the price of his coal fivefold.

Frick emerged from this crisis stronger and more emboldened than ever. Judge Mellon rewarded his acumen in 1876 with a credit line of $100,000. Mellon also introduced the entrepreneur to his own son Andrew. The younger Mellon, six years Frick's junior, was known for being socially removed and for living with his parents. Andrew, however, was so struck by Frick that the two became close friends and business partners.

The Mellons were not the only eminent Pittsburgh industrialists to take note of the young Frick. Accordion to Quentin Skrabec's work, Andrew Carnegie noted to his partners in Pittsburgh: "We must attach this young man Frick to our concern. He has great ability and great energy. Moreover, he has the coke—and we need it."

In 1884, Carnegie convinced Frick to have lunch with him and his mother in New York, where Frick was honeymooning with his new wife. After touring the city, including walking across the latest Carnegie steel structure—the Brooklyn Bridge—the couple met with Andrew and Mrs. Carnegie. Frick and Carnegie were able to successfully grow their joint coke and steel business over the next decades.

The financial and personal lives of Frick and Mellon also continued to intertwine, as their political, social, and business proclivities became indistinguishable. According to Mellon biographer David Cannadine, they regularly lunched together at Pittsburgh's Duquesne Club. To celebrate Frick's becoming a millionaire, they set out to Europe together to educate themselves on art and European society. In addition to the sheer amount of time the two shared in each other's company, their friendship revealed itself in the vast capital the Mellons entrusted to Frick—his personal loans from Mellon Bank amounted to $148,000 in 1885.

In 1887, Andrew Mellon and his brother purchased a portion of the Overholt Distillery, which had expanded production earlier in the decade so that it was producing an extraordinary 3,450 gallons of whiskey per day. Old Overholt Whiskey continued to flourish, and other manufacturers tried to cash in on the premium by incorporating flavor additives known as "Pittsburg Rye Essence" and "Monongahela Essence" to their neutral alcohols.

Mellon and Frick also used their prized whiskey as a political lubricant, bribing the Republican leadership with bottles of Old Overholt and contributing to a notoriously corrupt political machine that favored business interests above labor.

In 1899, the Broadford Distillery was rebuilt. Additional barrelhouses were added to accommodate an increasing supply of Old Farm Rye Whiskey, with the capacity to move through thirty-seven tons of grain per week. The expansion was completed in 1905, just fourteen years before the onset of Prohibition. Through the growth of the distillery, Mellon and Frick's friendship continued to flourish. By 1902, Frick was a major shareholder and director of the Mellon National Bank.

By 1917, it was clear that the federal government was getting ready to take on alcohol, and Mellon became anxious about the future of his and Frick's whiskey business. On October 28, 1919, the Volstead Act, or the National Prohibition Act, was enacted. Within five weeks, Frick, America's Coke King and the owner of America's original brand of rye whiskey, died of a heart attack at the age of sixty-nine. Mellon, his closest friend and business partner, became trustee to Frick's estate, gaining control over America's most legendary distillery.

Mellon's interest in the Overholt Distillery became problematic when he was appointed secretary of the treasury under President Harding in 1921. In his new Cabinet position, Mellon was, in effect, the United States' chief prohibition agent. And in a remarkable twist of history, it was the same position Alexander Hamilton had occupied when his whiskey tax inspired Abraham Overholt to start Old Farm Pure Rye Whiskey.

Mellon took reluctantly to his alcohol enforcement duties. He believed Prohibition was draconian and ineffective, and rightly felt that the Treasury Department was incapable of enforcing such a broad law. Furthermore, the teetotaling philosophies of Prohibition's proponents were a far cry from his personal interests. So Mellon did what any creative politician would do. He granted his Overholt Distillery one of the few medicinal whiskey licenses that were available to existing distilleries. Throughout Prohibition, the Overholt Distillery continued filling barrels with thousands of gallons of whiskey. Some was sold by prescription for medicinal "needs," but much of it likely found its way to the occasional speakeasy as well.

Ultimately, Mellon disposed of the politically troublesome distillery in 1925, selling all of his interest to an investor. Schenley Distillers, another Pittsburgh distillery, purchased Overholt's remaining whiskey stores, and National Distillers Inc. purchased the Overholt Distillery brand. The brand then transferred to Jim Beam in 1987. The whiskey Beam produces, made with a high-corn mash and on a continuous still, is a distant cousin of the original American whiskey that Abraham Overholt, Henry Clay Frick, and Andrew Mellon would have made on their copper pot stills in western Pennsylvania. The brand, however, remains the longest-running thread between pre-Prohibition American whiskey and the bourbon-centric American whiskey industry of today. Years before Pittsburgh was a steel town, it was a whiskey town. And years before America's whiskey was Kentucky bourbon, it was Pittsburgh Monongahela rye.

CHAPTER 3

THE STATE OF THE INDUSTRY

Today there is a new generation of whiskey makers that has begun and will continue to change the American spirits industry in the coming decades. In many ways, these upstart distillers are closer in spirit to the whiskey makers of the eighteenth and nineteenth centuries than they are to the predominant whiskey companies of today—though instead of attacking politicians with tar and feathers, they are lobbying states to change laws to allow for direct access to consumers.

While there were a handful of very early pioneers in modern craft distilling—especially in California—what we now know as the burgeoning craft industry didn't get its sea legs and enjoy significant new entrants until the early twenty-first century. Over the past two decades, the distilling industry has grown at a nearly exponential pace. The number of active distilleries in the United States nearly tripled between 2007 and 2013 alone, expanding from 564 distilleries to 1,501. And there are no signs of a slowdown. So far the industry has grown just as quickly as craft brewing—craft spirits were just a couple decades later to the game.

The very early years of the craft spirits industry saw clusters of small distilleries start up in California, Oregon, and Washington; states with the most amenable legal environments and the highest consumer interest in craft beer and wine. The earliest craft distillers tended toward brandy and eaux de vie, distilled wines and fruit brandies, which made sense given the West Coast's agricultural bounty of grapes and other fruits. New York State also became home to a relatively early community of craft distilleries as a result of the Farm Distillery Act passed in 2007, which created a fertile environment for fifteen new distilleries to start. As other states outside of the country's main wine regions have started distilling, the American craft-spirits industry has shifted its focus from brandies distilled from fruits and grapes to whiskeys distilled from grains.

Just as the number of players in the industry has grown, so has Americans' interest in rediscovering spirits. The number of Americans reporting that they've consumed bourbon, rye, or blended whiskey in the past thirty days increased by 40 percent from 2008 to 2014. Now an estimated 27 million Americans enjoy a glass of whiskey in a given month. Some of this growth is coming from former beer drinkers, as people switch out their pints for cocktails and drams; from 2005 to 2011, beer servings fell 1.7 percent in America, while spirit servings grew a remarkable 15 percent.

Just as in the craft beer world, it is the small brands that are driving growth in the spirits industry. For example, the gin market experienced 1.6 percent growth between 2013 and 2014, and an astonishing 45 percent of that growth came from small brands, which outstripped the growth of the large brands by nearly nineteen times. Over the past two decades, this trend holds true across all spirit categories. The shares of the top five spirit brands in straight whiskey, scotch, vodka, gin, rum, and tequila have eroded over the last twenty years, giving way to smaller brands.

Spirit Category	Top 5 Brand Market Share Loss, 1993-2013 as Revenue as % of category	Small Brand Market Share Growth, 1993-2013 as Revenue as % of category
Straight Whiskey	-17	+12
Scotch Whiskey	-40	+30
Vodka	-48	+37
Gin	-36	+29
Rum	-32	+24
Tequila	-54	+21

Source: Harry Kohlmann, Craft Market Strategies, slides 10 & 11

As the farm-to-table, organic, and natural foods movements continue to pervade our national mindset, consumers are seeking out authentic and small production methods for many of their foods and beverages. Consumers have shifted to smaller brands in categories seemingly removed from spirits, such as popcorn, oils, nuts, dried fruits, salad dressings, and peanut butters. Even the frozen food aisle—that beacon of American big-branded convenience food—has seen a shift toward smaller brands.

This could be an alarming reality for many large spirit companies who have been sitting in relatively hegemonic comfort for decades. As late as 2013, the top five spirit conglomerates—Diageo, Bacardi USA, Beam Inc., Pernod Ricard USA, and

Brown Forman—held approximately 60 percent of the total American spirits market. Consumers, long complacent with the consolidation and static quality of the American distilling industry, now seem to be restless with those same big brands.

This restlessness is likely a part of the same pendulum that swings back and forth between fragmentation and consolidation in most industries. Prior to Prohibition, American distilling was almost unimaginably fragmented. The United States was home to thousands of distilleries, which ranged widely in terms of production scale. In the years since, the industry has shifted to the other extreme of significant consolidation. Michael Kinstlick's impressive graph shows that after years of a highly competitive market in the late nineteenth and early twentieth centuries, the industry big boys enjoyed more than seventy years of a winner-take-all market:

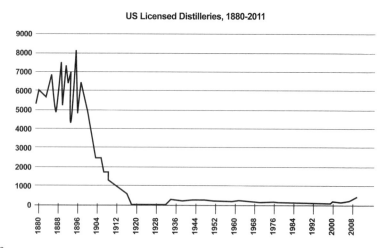

US Licensed Distilleries, 1880-2011

This consolidated landscape resulted from a mix of technological, legal, and economic forces that happened in three major shifts. The first big shift came with the introduction of the modern industrial still, or the Coffey still, which spread through the country beginning in the 1830s. This still mechanized much of the distillation process, and is now standard in large American distilleries. The invention of this still also shifted production from the traditional copper-pot still, which was used to produce Monongahela rye.

The benefit of the Coffey still was that it greatly increased efficiency and consistency. With vast improvements in these areas, the industry didn't need numerous, inefficient pot stills dotting the landscape. The downside to this industrial still was that it sacrificed flavor and nuance between various regions and various batches of whiskey. With the modern industrial still, we moved from being a country with *tens* of thousands of pot stills to a country with just thousands, and many of those became the mechanized, continuous variety.

The second big shift that led to wider consolidation was, of course, Prohibition, which flatlined legal distilleries until 1936, when only a small number were able to rebound. By now, we're all aware how ineffectual Prohibition was at preventing alcohol consumption in the United States. It was, however, extremely effective at consolidating the distilling industry into the hands of its biggest players. Those with the deepest pockets were able to wait out the more than decade-long dry spell, absorbing the liquid, brand, and equipment assets of the companies that went under. And these big players came out of Prohibition all the stronger. These included the largest spirits company, National Distillers Products Corporation, which purchased the older Overholt stores of whiskey and emerged from Prohibition as an industry behemoth. Prohibition also effectively reduced the quality of American whiskey for many years, as suppliers had to develop creative ways to maximize their limited supplies of aged whiskey, stretching it with water, neutral alcohol, food coloring, and other flavors to get more mileage out of what they had left in storage.

The final shift towards consolidation was caused by something less obvious, and that has to do with the way spirits sales are structured in the United States. American spirits are sold in a three-tier system: there are suppliers, the people who put the spirits in bottles; wholesalers, the people with the warehouses and trucks who get the spirits from the suppliers to the retailers; and retailers who sell to the whiskey-consuming public. As the American spirits suppliers began consolidating, they wielded great power, and the distributors began consolidating in response. And while many of these distributors may have started as regional family businesses, they've had to become just as national and consolidated as the suppliers they represent.

Distributors are a spirits maker's only way to get her products to market in states that do not allow small distilleries to sell directly to consumers. Distributors also have an interest in protecting their national brands against the smaller upstarts. Southern Wine and Spirits, one of the nation's largest distributors, for example, raked in $10 billion in 2012. And upwards of 40 percent of a distributor's revenue can come from a *single* supplier.

Currently, there are a limited number of distributors that will work with small distilleries, which creates a daunting barrier for small producers trying to reach a retail environment. This is why direct-to-consumer legislation, like that which exists in Michigan, New York, and Pennsylvania, is so critical to the future health of the craft spirits industry.

All of these historical, commercial, and economic developments have ultimately led to a fairly staid and singular mix of consumer offerings. If we take Pennsylvania as a case study, we can see how consolidation has played out on the shelf. Pennsylvania is an important state for whiskey makers. It ranks fifth in spirit consumption in the nation, consuming more than 3 percent of the nation's spirits, behind only California, Florida, New York, and Texas. It's also the largest single liquor purchaser in the country. Because of this, manufacturers devote significant resources to the offerings in this state. Yet in 2013, a full 98 percent of American whiskey sold in the state of Pennsylvania was just one type—corn whiskey, or bourbon— produced by a small handful of companies. In the very same state where Monongahela rye whiskey originated, less than 2 percent of the whiskey sold was made from rye grain.

And it only gets worse. Because if you break down where that 2 percent of rye whiskey came from, you can see that the vast majority came from just two distilleries. One, Beam Suntori, you probably have heard of, but the other, called Midwest Grain Products, or MGP, you might not know about. Headquartered in Lawrenceburg, Indiana, MGP is one of the largest distilleries (by gallon production) in America. MGP turns out lots of rye whiskey as well as vodka, known in the industry as Grain Neutral Spirit or GNS, and bioplastics. Turns out they made about 40 percent of the rye whiskey sold in Pennsylvania in 2013, leaving Beam to make most of the rest.

MGP and Beam ryes are bottled under a variety of different labels. So even when there really isn't a heck of a lot of choice for consumers, the companies can create the illusion of choice. For all intents and purposes, that meant whiskey buyers in Pennsylvania were left with only two rye whiskeys to choose from: Beam or MGP.

This bulk rye certainly gets around in the industry. Craft distillers, as well as companies that bottle whiskey, regularly receive emails from America's bulk whiskey suppliers. In 2015, they offered to sell their bulk rye whiskey from $3.66 to $4.09 per bottle. That's a good deal; there's some nice room for margin between $4 bulk whiskey and a $30 to $50 price tag on the shelf. But it just goes to show how the American rye whiskey industry is one that has profited from consumer confusion and obfuscation and a whole lot of clever marketing.

An industry with just two dominant suppliers is not a healthy or interesting one from a consumer perspective. An industry in this kind of shape is one that's begging for companies whose margins are built on consumer education, not on consumer confusion. This is the argument for grain-to-bottle, craft spirits.

It may be hard now to imagine our country filled with tens of thousands of distilleries—a world where different regions produced their own distinctive style of whiskey or spirit. At the turn of the twentieth century, America had a distillery for every 9,500 citizens. These days, even with the current boom in small distilleries, there is a distillery for every 210,000. In a mid-size city like Pittsburgh, this is the difference between having one distillery versus having thirty-two. So in spite of the hordes of new entrants into distilling, and the growth of small brands, we still have a long way to go to come close to pre-Prohibition levels of diversity in the American distilling landscape. With 1,400 craft distilleries in America and counting, we are certainly making progress. And as curious drinkers renew their interest in lost styles of American spirits, we are on the brink of a sea change in American distilling.

The burgeoning consumer demand for craft spirits will continue to eat away at the consolidated supplier market. Some people in the industry anticipate a day in which the top twenty spirits brands will carry half of the spirits market, while the remaining half will be split among a multitude of craft brands. This will force distributors and suppliers to change their current mindset. Instead of looking for the next big national brand, suppliers may look to embrace regionality in their sales and marketing and acquisition strategies.

If this is the state of the spirits world we're looking at ten or twenty years from now, we should probably get a good handle on what craft spirits are exactly. While it seems like a simple question, the definition of craft in American whiskey is, perhaps, the most central and nuanced issue facing distillers and consumers today.

CHAPTER 4

THE REBIRTH OF CRAFT

Over the course of this short book, we've sped through the long trajectory of rye whiskey's history in America. Whiskey began as a necessity in the frontier economy of western Pennsylvania, then grew into a national force that fueled twentieth-century American industry, before suddenly crashing with Prohibition, to be largely erased from our national consciousness. Today, craft distilleries represent an opportunity to regain this lost heritage and rediscover the regional diversity of American spirits.

At the heart of the current boom in craft distilling are consumers who are seeking authenticity and spirits that reflect the place they come from. But what is a craft spirit exactly? Do you know it when you taste it? When you see it? These are questions that have divided people in the current craft community.

In fact, the question of what makes a craft spirit brought three separate lawsuits against one company, Templeton Rye, which has represented itself as a craft distiller. Once featured on

National Public Radio as a darling of the craft rye renaissance, Templeton became an industry lightning rod. While the company itself marketed its rye whiskey as an Iowa rye—made in small batches using a family Prohibition-era recipe—it turns out it was sourcing its rye from Midwest Grain Products. MGP, as America's largest supplier of rye whiskey, has built its operation on continuous industrial distillation; it doesn't produce its whiskey in small batches. It's also located in Indiana, a geographically inconvenient fact for a whiskey company claiming to be from Iowa.

After Templeton achieved national distribution and strong sales, consumers began asking questions, which ultimately resulted in a number of class-action lawsuits claiming that the company deceived consumers. In July 2015, Templeton settled all the suits for an undisclosed amount. The company was forced to set aside a cash reserve to refund customers who had purchased bottles under false pretenses.

The Templeton case is a clear case of consumer deception, but the question of what exactly makes a craft spirit often sits in a much grayer zone. It's a question that has created contentious debate in the beer and wine industries for decades. The Craft Brewers Association has gone out on a limb and created a definition for the kind of work they do: "An American craft brewer is small, independent, and traditional." The association then goes on to define each of those adjectives. "Small" means an annual production of not more than 6 million barrels of beer, which, at about 3 percent of America's annual beer sales, leaves quite a bit of room for growth for most small brewers.

"Independent" means that less than a quarter of the brewery is owned or controlled by an external interest. And finally, a "traditional" craft brewer creates "a majority of its total beverage alcohol volume in beers whose flavors derive from traditional or innovative brewing ingredients and their fermentation."

For spirits, the conversation around craft at this early stage in the industry is rapidly evolving, but it's much more basic. For the first several years that the industry trade group, the American Craft Spirits Association, existed, the big question concerning craft was simple: Do you make the stuff yourself or do you buy it from a larger manufacturer and then bottle and label it? If you are a bottler, then you should not pretend to be otherwise on your label. But this would not necessarily disqualify you from being a "craft" producer.

However, as the craft spirits industry continues to mature, patience for bottlers of bulk spirits appears to be waning among both consumers and professionals in the industry. Collectively, the craft spirit industry is coming around to the notion that the only way to return to the dynamic, regionally-driven spirits landscape that existed pre-Prohibition is for distilleries to make things themselves, preferably from local ingredients.

This is the primary hallmark of craft distilling. By fermenting and distilling ingredients—grains, sugar, fruit, molasses, honey—from their own regions, small distillers bring a needed diversity and regionality to the distilled-spirits landscape. This local sourcing and grain-to-bottle production methodology is the heart and soul of craft distilling. This is the same kind of production that led to a rich array of regionally-specific spirits in the past—Monongahela rye versus Maryland rye versus Kentucky bourbon, for example. This "taste of place," or *terroir*, is precisely what created such dynamic and varied American whiskeys in the past, which makes it the central attribute of craft distilling today.

A second hallmark of craft distilling is a dedication to education and transparency. If craft distillers are going to succeed, they have to create an educated and curious consumer base. This principle guides distribution strategy—leading to tasting rooms with direct sales to consumers—and perhaps most importantly, consumer engagement methodologies, including lots of tours and education events.

One thing is clear: if you're going to invest in making your consumers really smart about what they're drinking, they're going to start asking lots of questions. And so, craft distilleries must operate with higher standards around transparency and consumer engagement. A company's value should grow as consumer understanding grows. This focus on education and transparency is a marked turn for the spirits industry, which has previously reveled in marketing mythology.

The third hallmark of a craft spirit is a resource-intensive focus on innovation. This is definitely an exciting time to be a spirits drinker. With 1,500 distilleries playing around with craft spirits in different ways, there is a tremendous amount of new expressions to try across all categories, and those who claim to be an expert on anything these days are making a big claim.

Harry Kohlman, an industry consultant, charted the number of new spirit label filings per year to the Alcohol and Tobacco Tax Trade Bureau, and found that from 2002 to 2013, the annual number of labels filed had more than tripled. A.C. Nielsen data backs up this trend, showing a 27 percent growth in the number of spirits on shelves in early 2017 versus four years prior.

This focus on innovation can be a sticky wicket in an industry as tradition-driven as whiskey. After all, the primary message the industry has communicated to consumers over the past fifty years has been all about how long something has been sitting in a barrel. A whiskey's age is important, but it's also an aspect of distilling that's relatively simple to communicate—it's easy to post a number on a bottle and mark the price up accordingly. Broadening the conversation beyond the barrel—to include fermentation and distillation methodologies, and the types of grains, malts, botanicals, and yeasts used—requires much more consumer education and curiosity.

The fourth and final hallmark of craft distilling is inclusivity. As you've likely noticed, American whiskey, in its most recent history, has suffered from a narrow communication strategy. When we began working on our distillery in 2010 and talked to people about what they thought of when they thought of whiskey, the image we heard most frequently was of an older gentleman, sitting on a leather couch, smoking a cigar. While entirely understandable, this is a strangely anachronistic and narrow view of whiskey. For most of its long history, whiskey was a drink of the people—of all the people. If you were attending a wedding, a funeral, or even having lunch, you were very often drinking whiskey—man or woman, rich or poor.

Modern whiskey aisles do not reflect whiskey's true democratic roots. They are filled with brown parchment, hunting scenes, and language aimed at a very particular audience—a club that many consumers do not feel a part of. Much of the work of the craft industry is to make whiskey relevant again for all those people who strongly believe that it is not for them. And if the industry can successfully do that, it will have an enormous population to drink with. Today's craft distillers are interested in telling this story; opening whiskey up to a wider audience has the potential to yield great returns.

Now, in none of the above hallmarks have we tried to define the word "craft." It is a word that is now applied so liberally that it risks becoming meaningless. In 2014 alone, the word "handcrafted" appeared on bar and restaurant menus 68 percent more often by the end of the year than it had in the first two quarters. And in the distilling world, the word "craft" is bandied about all over the place. Right now, consumers have been left to figure out exactly what that word means to them.

Certainly there are distilleries that identify as craft that rely on commodity grains, that do not focus on innovation, that are still focused on the old man with the cigar at the expense of the rest of the population, or that don't spend much time thinking about or developing consumer education. But taken as a whole, the attributes of modern craft spirits—small-scale production from regional ingredients, consumer engagement, innovation, and inclusivity—are driving the craft renaissance.

Perhaps as importantly, each of these hallmarks were part and parcel of American spirits in the past. And as the industry's pendulum swings back toward smaller, regional producers, the renaissance in American whiskey is truly a *rebirth* of craft. We, as whiskey drinkers, should not take this for granted. Who knows how many decades we have until the strong pull of consolidation swings the pendulum back? But for now, let's revel in whiskeys packed with the flavor of their place—produced on the pot stills we can see up close by the people who work with regional farmers.

THE PROCESS

START WITH ORGANIC GRAIN FROM LOCAL FARMS

TO CONTINUE A JOURNEY FROM GRAIN TO BOTTLE

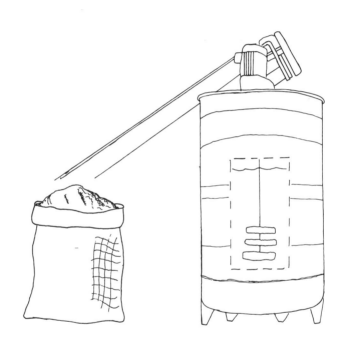

**GRAIN IS GROUND INTO GRIST AND TURNED INTO A
MASH IN THE MASH TUN**

MASH IS TRANSFERRED TO THE FERMENTERS AND FERMENTS FOR FOUR DAYS

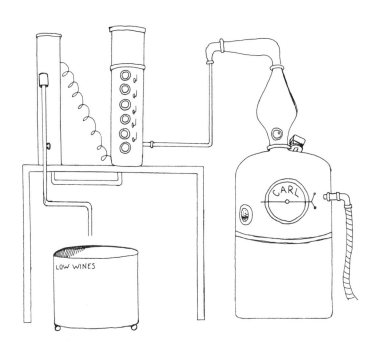

FERMENTED BEER IS DISTILLED TWO TIMES TO 110 TO 125 PROOF

DISTILLED WHISKEY IS BARRELED INTO NEW CHARRED OAK BARRELS

BARRELED WHISKEY IS AGED IN THE BARRELHOUSE ONE TO FIVE YEARS

**THEN EMPTIED AND PROOFED WITH WATER
IN STAINLESS STEEL HOLDING TANKS**

AND BOTTLED AND CORKED BY HAND FOUR AT A TIME

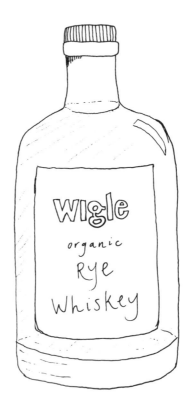

EACH BOTTLE IS HAND LABELED

wigle rye Manhattan   Sherry darlin'   Strawberry Shrub

AND READY FOR CRAFTING COCKTAILS OR DRINKING NEAT

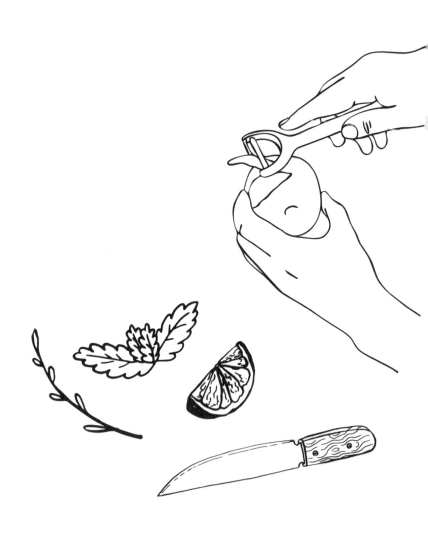

COCKTAIL RECIPES

STRAWBERRY SHRUB
ANGELA SMALLEY NEMACOLIN WOODLANDS

Origins in seventeenth-century England where vinegar was used as an alternative to citrus juices in the preservation of berries and other fruits for the off seasons.

2 oz. Wigle Organic Straight Monongahela Rye Whiskey

2 oz. strawberry shrub syrup*

½ oz. lemon juice

1 oz. soda water

Garnish with lemon zest and fresh black pepper

NOTES: Add the rye whiskey and strawberry shrub syrup in a shaker with ice. Shake, then add lemon juice and soda water. Strain into a martini glass; Garnish with lemon zest, and fresh ground black pepper.

*Strawberry Shrub Syrup
In a bowl, let three cups sugar and zest of three lemons rest for one hour before pressing zest to release oils. Remove zest and pour the sugar over a bowl of four cups of strawberries, hulled and quartered. Place lid on bowl and set aside in refrigerator for two days. It is ready when the syrup has formed and the berries have turned to pulp. In a glass jar, strain the strawberries leaving only the syrup. Add one cup balsamic vinegar, one cup white vinegar, and one cup champagne vinegar to syrup, and store in a refrigerator for three days. Shake occasionally to help the sugar dissolve.

WAR OF CONQUESTS

CECIL USHER BUTCHER & THE RYE

Name is inspired by the French-Indian War. The French would call these battles the war of the conquest. The cocktail has two French ingredients, dry (French) vermouth and absinthe and then American staples rye and apples. Enjoy!

1 oz. Wigle Organic Straight Monongahela Rye Whiskey

1 oz. Wigle Apple Brandy

¾ oz. dry vermouth

¼oz. demerara syrup

1 dash Wigle Organic Pomander Orange Bitters

1 dash Wigle Aromatic Bitters

Rinse of Wigle Absent Minded Absinthe

NOTES: Add first six ingredients to a mixing glass and stir until properly chilled and diluted. Pour a small amount of absinthe in a rocks glass and swirl to coat and dump excess out. Add one large ice cube to glass and pour contents of mixing glass. Garnish with a twist of orange peel expressed over the top and dropped into the drink. Cheers.

SHERRY DARLIN'
DREW CRANISKY INDEPENDENT BREWING COMPANY

**2 oz. Wigle Organic Straight Monongahela Rye Whiskey
(or another bonded-strength rye)**

¾ oz. Pedro Ximénez sherry

¼ oz. Luxardo maraschino cherries

2 dashes Angostura bitters

1 dash mole bitters

GLASS: coupe

GARNISH: orange twist

NOTES: Combine all ingredients in a mixing glass. Stir to chill. Strain into a chilled coupe and garnish with an orange twist. with a generous scoop of ice, and strain over fresh ice into a rocks glass. We recommend Pittsburgh Seltzer Works and fresh juice.

WIGLE RYE MANHATTAN

DAWN YOUNG BAR MANAGER AT THE SPEAKEASY AT
THE OMNI WILLIAM PENN HOTEL.

**1 ½ oz. Wigle Organic White Monongahela Rye
Whiskey**

½ oz. Dolin Blanc

½ oz. cherry juice

GARNISH: Luxardo cherry

NOTES: We serve the Rye Manhattan two way—in a
coupe glass with a slightly torched orange garnish,
simple and sip-able, or over one large cube in a
traditional rocks glass. We find that using the
Wigle Rye and the Dolin Blanc vermouth is what
sets this Manhattan apart from other recipes. The
rye is very clean, has good toasted nut flavor, and
a slightly oaky note on the palate. In addition to
its intriguing flavor, the color of this Manhattan is
stunning, and the luxardo cherry compliments the
rye, adding a dark cherry pucker to the finish.

SUMMERSET

1 ½ oz. Wigle Organic White Monongahela Rye Whiskey

2 oz. pomegranate juice

4 oz. ginger beer

GLASS: Collins

GARNISH: pomegranate berries

NOTES: Measure and pour all ingredients in the glass, top with a generous scoop of ice, and gently stir. We prefer POM Pomegranate juice and Natrona Jamaica's Finest Ginger Beer.

WHISKEY DAISY

1 ½ oz. Wigle Organic White Monongahela Rye Whiskey

¾ oz. Yellow Chartreuse

¾ oz. lemon juice

Splash of chilled seltzer

GLASS: rocks

GARNISH: half-rim of salt

NOTES: Prep the salt-rimmed glass ahead of time. Measure all ingredients carefully, vigorously shake with a generous scoop of ice, and strain over fresh ice into a rocks glass. We recommend Pittsburgh Seltzer Works and fresh juice.

MAPLE WHISKEY SOUR

2 oz. Wigle Organic White Wheat Whiskey

½ oz. lemon juice

½ oz. orange juice

½ oz. Grade B maple syrup

2 dashes Wigle Organic Pomander Orange Bitters

GLASS: rocks

GARNISH: orange slice

NOTES: Measure all ingredients carefully, vigorously shake with a generous scoop of ice, and strain over fresh ice into a rocks glass. We recommend both fresh juices and real maple syrup—it's worth it.

MILK PUNCH

2 oz. Wigle Allegheny Wheat Whiskey

1 tbsp. simple syrup

6 oz. whole milk

GLASS: Collins

GARNISH: shaved nutmeg

NOTES: Measure all ingredients carefully, vigorously shake with a generous scoop of ice, and strain over fresh ice into a Collins glass.

WHISKEY BUCK

1 ½ oz. Wigle Allegheny Wheat Whiskey

Juice of ½ lemon

4 oz. ginger beer

GLASS: Collins

GARNISH: spent lemon hull

NOTES: Measure and pour all ingredients in the Collins glass, top with a generous scoop of ice, and gently stir. We prefer Natrona Jamaica's Finest Ginger Beer.

WHISKEY BRAMBLE

2 oz. Wigle Allegheny Wheat Whiskey

3 blackberries (muddled)

¾ oz. lemon juice

½ oz. demerara syrup

GLASS: rocks

GARNISH: lemon twist and blackberry

NOTES: There are two ways to make this. The first is to build the entire drink in the rocks glass, with the muddled blackberries at the bottom (do this if you like small bits of fresh berries in your cocktail). The second is to muddle the berries in a shaker, measure and pour the remaining ingredients, vigorously shake with a generous scoop of ice, and fine-strain over fresh ice.

DON DRAPER'S DUVET

(HOT) 8 servings

12 oz Wigle Organic Straight Monongahela Rye Whiskey

1 qt. apple cider

2 tbsp. honey

2 cinnamon sticks

2 allspice berries

½ apple, thinly sliced

NOTES: Mull the spices, honey, apple slices, and cider together on medium heat for fifteen minutes.
Add the whiskey and serve immediately.

WHISKEY SOUR

2 oz. Wigle Organic Straight Monongahela Rye Whiskey

¾ oz. lemon juice

¾ oz. demerara syrup

2 dashes aromatic bitters

Egg white (optional)

GLASS: coupe

GARNISH: bitters dropped on top

NOTES: Measure all ingredients carefully, vigorously shake with a generous scoop of ice, and strain into a chilled coupe. We prefer making this with an egg white (it helps make a wonderfully frothy texture), but it's certainly not necessary. Same applies to the bitters—we just love the little addition of flavor and aroma.

WARD 8

2 oz Wigle Organic Straight Monongahela Rye Whiskey

¾ oz. lemon juice

¾ oz. orange juice

1 tsp. pomegranate grenadine

GLASS: coupe

GARNISH: lemon peel

NOTES: Measure all ingredients carefully, vigorously shake with a generous scoop of ice, and strain in a chilled coupe. We recommend both fresh juices and real pomegranate grenadine—it's worth it.

GIN AND JUICE

1 ½ oz. Wigle Organic Ginever

2 oz. grapefruit juice

2 oz. orange juice

GLASS: rocks

GARNISH: lime wedge

NOTES: Measure all ingredients carefully, vigorously shake with a generous scoop of ice, and strain over fresh ice into a rocks glass. Squeeze a lime wedge over the top and drop in. We recommend using fresh juices, and specifically ruby red grapefruits—it's worth it.

SOUTHSIDE

2 oz. Wigle Organic Ginever

¾ oz. lime juice

¾ oz. simple syrup

7-10 mint leaves

GLASS: coupe

GARNISH: mint sprig

NOTES: Measure all ingredients carefully, vigorously shake with a generous scoop of ice, and double strain over fresh ice into a chilled coupe. We recommend using fresh juice and spearmint instead of peppermint.

GIN FIZZ

2 oz. Wigle Organic Ginever

¾ oz. lemon juice

¾ oz. simple syrup

1 egg white

Splash of soda water

GLASS: Collins

GARNISH: lime wedge

NOTES: Hold the soda water until the last step. Measure all ingredients carefully, vigorously shake *without* ice until everything is incorporated. Add a generous scoop of ice and shake again until well-chilled. Strain into an ice-free Collins glass and top with the soda water to form a foamy top.

IMPROVED HOLLAND GIN COCKTAIL

2 oz. Wigle Organic Barrel-Rested Ginever

1 tsp. simple syrup

1 tsp. maraschino liqueur

2 dashes Wigle Organic Pomander Orange Bitters

GLASS: rocks

GARNISH: lemon twist

NOTES: Measure all ingredients carefully, pouring them into a stirring glass. Add a generous scoop of ice and stir until well-chilled. Strain into a rocks glass over fresh ice, garnish with a large lemon twist. We recommend Lazzaroni maraschino liqueur for this, but Luxardo also works well.

DUTCH NEGRONI

1 oz. Wigle Organic Barrel-Rested Ginever

1 oz. Campari

1 oz. sweet vermouth

GLASS: coupe

GARNISH: orange twist

NOTES: Measure all ingredients carefully, pouring them into a stirring glass. Add a generous scoop of ice and stir until very well-chilled. Strain into a chilled coupe glass and garnish with a large orange twist. We recommend Dolin sweet vermouth for this, but Martini and Rossi also works well.

BIBLIOGRAPHY

Chapter 1: The Whiskey Rebellion

Brackenridge, H.M. *History of the Western Insurrection in Western Pennsylvania: Commonly Called the Whiskey Insurrection 1794.* Pittsburgh: W.S. Haven, 1859.

Craig, Neville B. *The History of Pittsburgh: With a Brief Notice of Its Facilities of Communication and Other Advantages for Commercial and Manufacturing Purposes.* Pittsburgh: J.H. Mellor, 1851.

Hogeland, William. *The Whiskey Rebellion: George Washington, Alexander Hamilton, and the Frontier Rebels Who Challenged America's Newfound Sovereignty.* New York: Scribner, 2006.

Findley, William. *History of the Insurrection in the Four Western Counties of Pennsylvania in the Year, MDCCXCIV.* Philadelphia: Samuel Harrison Smith, 1796.

Knight, David C. *The Whiskey Rebellion, 1794: Revolt in Pennsylvania Threatens American Unity.* New York: Franklin Watts, Inc, 1968.

Morse, Jr., John T. *The Jeffersonian Democracy: Albert Gallatin.* American Statesman. V.13. Boston: Houghton, Mifflin, and Company, 1898.

Mulkearn, Lois. "Pittsburgh in 1806." *Pitt: A Quarterly of Fact and Thought at the University of Pittsburgh.* Spring 1948.

Pittsburgh Gazette, 1791-1794.

Slaughter, Thomas P. *The Whiskey Rebellion: Frontier Epilogue to the American Revolution.* New York: Oxford University Press, 1986.

Swauger, Mary Pat. *Insurrection! A Short History of the Whiskey Rebellion of 1794 and its Connection with Sons of Oliver Miller of Western Pennsylvania.* South Park, Penn.: Oliver Miller Homestead Associates,1993.

Wall, Elizabeth J. *Men of the Whiskey Insurrection in Southwestern Pennsylvania.* Pittsburgh: E.J. Wall, 1988.

Washington, George. "Proclamation-Cessation of Violence and Obstruction of Justice in Protest of Liquor Laws," September 15, 1792, From *Spark's Washington*, Vol X, p. 532, as published in The Avalon Project, Yale Law School.

Washington, George. "Proclamation," February 24, 1794, as published in *Founders Online from Gazette of the United States and Evening Advertiser*, Philadelphia, February 26, 1794.

Chapter 2: A Love Story

Anonymous. *A. Overholt & Co., Inc: A History of the Company and of the Overholt Family.* August 1940. Pennsylvania Room, Carnegie Library of Pittsburgh.

Cannadine, David. *Mellon: An American Life.* New York: Alfred A. Knopf, 2006.

United States Department of the Interior. National Park Service. *National Register of Historic Places Multiple Property Documentation Form for Whiskey Rebellion Resources in Southwestern Pennsylvania.* PA Historical & Museum Commission, September 21, 1992. Print.

Harvey, George. *Henry Clay Frick: The Man.* Washington DC: BeardBooks, 1928.

Heald, Sarah H., eds; United States Department of the Interior. National Park Service. *Historic American Buildings Survey/Historic American Engineering Record.* Washington, DC, 1990. Web. May 2015. https://www.nps.gov/HDP/.

Library of Congress. *Historic American Buildings Survey: West Overton.* HABS No. PA-5654. Print. Accessed via Pennsylvania Department, Carnegie Library of Pittsburgh, 8 May 2015.

Koskoff, David E. *The Mellons: The Chronicle of America's Richest Family.* New York: Thomas Y. Crowell Company, 1978.

Critchfield Overholt, Karen Rose. "Old Overholt: The History of a Whiskey." www.*Karensbranches.com.* 10 Dec. 2005. Web. 21 May 2015.

Mellon, James. *The Judge: A life of Thomas Mellon, Founder of a Fortune.* New Haven: Yale University Press, 2011.

Mellon, Thomas. *Thomas Mellon and His Times.* Pittsburgh and London: University of Pittsburgh Press, 1994.

Oliver, John W., "Henry Clay Frick, Pioneer-Patriot and Philanthropist, 1849-1919," *The Western Pennsylvania Historical Magazine* 32 no. 3-4. September 1949.

Sanborn's Surveys of the Whiskey Warehouses of Pennsylvania, West Virginia, Maryland, New Jersey and New York. New York: Sanborn Perris Map Co, 1894. Page 28: The Overholt works at Broadford, Fayette County. Accessed via Pennsylvania Department, Carnegie Library of Pittsburgh, 8 May 2015.

Sanger, Martha Frick Symington. *Henry Clay Frick: An Intimate Portrait.* New York: Abbeville Press Publishers, 1998.

Schmidlapp, Christina. "National Register of Historic Places Nomination Form for West Overton Historic District." 1985. Accessed via Pennsylvania Department, Carnegie Library of Pittsburgh, 8 May 2015.

Schreiner, Samuel A., Jr. *Henry Clay Frick: The Gospel of Greed.* New York: St. Martin's Press, 1995.

Skrabec, Quentin R. Jr. *Henry Clay Frick: The Life of a Perfect Capitalist.* Jefferson, NC: McFarland and Co., 2010.

United States Department of the Interior National Park Service, *National Register of Historic Places; Multiple Property Documentation From: Whiskey Rebellion Resources in Southwestern Pennsylvania; 1992.*

Washlaski, Raymond A. "The Abraham Overholt Distillery Building CA 1859 Drawing Portfolio." 1859. Accessed via Pennsylvania Department, Carnegie Library of Pittsburgh, 8 May 2015.

West Overton Village Pennsylvania: Schematic Design, Interpretive Prospectus, Environmental Assessment, c1994. Accessed via Pennsylvania Department, Carnegie Library of Pittsburgh, 8 May 2015.

Willis, H. Parker. "What Whiskey Is," *McClure's Magazine*, Vol. 34, pp 687-700, 1910.

Chapter 3: The State of the Industry

Distilled Spirits Council, Economic and Strategic Analysis. Washington DC, February 2015. http://www.discus.org/economics/highlights/. Web. August 2015.

Distilled Spirits Council, Economic and Strategic Analysis, *US Brandy/Cognac Market*, Washington DC, February 2014. http://www.discus.org/economics/highlights/. Web. August 2015.

Distilled Spirits Council, Economic and Strategic Analysis, *Cordials & Liqueurs*, Washington DC, February 2015. http://www.discus.org/economics/highlights/. Web. August 2015.

Distilled Spirits Council, Economic and Strategic Analysis, *Whiskeys of the Great White North*, Washington DC, February 2015. http://www.discus.org/economics/highlights/. Web. August 2015.

Distilled Spirits Council, Economic and Strategic Analysis, *Real Martinis are Made with Gin!*, Washington DC, February 2015. http://www.discus.org/economics/highlights/. Web. August 2015.

Distilled Spirits Council, Economic and Strategic Analysis, *Rum: If you like Pina Coladas*, Washington DC, February 2015. http://www.discus.org/economics/highlights/. Web. August 2015.

Distilled Spirits Council, Economic and Strategic Analysis, *Scotch: Take the High Road*, Washington DC, February 2015. http://www.discus.org/economics/highlights/. Web. August 2015.

Distilled Spirits Council, Economic and Strategic Analysis, *US Tequila Market*, Washington DC, February 2015. http://www.discus.org/economics/highlights/. Web. August 2015.

Distilled Spirits Council, Economic and Strategic Analysis, *Vodka: The Spirit of the Industry*, Washington DC, February 2015. http://www.discus.org/economics/highlights/. Web. August 2015.

Distilled Spirits Council, Economic and Strategic Analysis, *On America's Whiskey Trail,* Washington DC, February 2015. http://www.discus.org/economics/highlights/. Web. August 2015.

Distilled Spirits Council, *Apparent Consumption of Distilled Spirits by State in Wine Gallons: Preliminary Report,* Washington DC, February 2013. http://www.discus.org/economics/volume/. Web. August 2015.

Distilled Spirits Council, *Economic Contribution of Alcohol Beverage Industry,* Washington DC, 2010. http://www.discus.org/assets/1/7/ContributionFactSheet.pdf. Web. August 2015.

Kinstlick, Michael. *The US Craft Distilling Market: 2011 and Beyond.* http://www.coppersea.com/wp-content/uploads/2012/04/Craft_Distilling_2011_White_Paper_Final.pdf. May 2015.

Kohlmann, Ph.D., Harry. "Craft Market Strategies." American Distilling Institute Conference. Sheraton Hotel, Denver, CO. April 2013. Session Presentation.

Kohlmann, Ph.D., Harry. "Route to Market & Growth Acceleration" American Craft Spirits Association Conference. Sheraton Hotel, Denver, CO. March 2014. Session presentation.

Menashe, Jeff. "Why Craft Beer is Next." April 2013. Powerpoint presentation.

Menashe, Jeff. "State of the Wine Industry 2013." April 2013. Powerpoint presentation.

Menashe, Jeff. "State of the Craft Beer Industry 2013." April 2013. Powerpoint presentation.

Menashe, Jeff. "State of the Spirits Industry 2013." American Distilling Institute Conference. Sheraton Hotel, Denver, CO. April 2013. Session presentation.

Chapter 4: The Rebirth of Craft

Rodgers, Grant. *Des Moines Register*, "Templeton Rye reaches lawsuit settlement." July 13, 2015.

ACKNOWLEDGEMENTS

This book rests upon the work of the many passionate historians and volunteers who have captured the history of pre-Prohibition regional whiskey. We have tried to harness this collective recorded regional history and expand upon it in our modest way, knowing that our work is a small contribution to an ongoing history that is being written over decades. We hope that another whiskey lover will be inspired to take the next step and capture more of the pieces of Pennsylvania whiskey history (and beyond!) that we did not tend to in this brief book.

We appreciated visits from branches of the Wigle family from Pennsylvania, Canada, and West Virginia. Nadine Wigle Hoffman of West Virginia generously shared with us her family notebooks and her knowledge of the Wigle lineage.

Visits to and from staff at Whiskey Rebellion sites in western Pennsylvania—including the Presley Neville house, the Oliver Miller homestead, and the David Bradford house—were helpful in understanding the historic and ongoing importance of this episode in the history of western Pennsylvania and our regional identity.

Jessica Kadie-Barclay and the West Overton Village team have worked for years to tell the Overholt story, and have created a beautiful site that should be on any whiskey lovers must-visit list.

We cannot thank enough the librarians in the Pennsylvania Department at the Carnegie Library in Pittsburgh, especially Marilyn Holt, and the wonderful staff at the Heinz History Center for their patient help in identifying and accessing materials. A special thanks to Andy Masich, Sandra Smith, Leslie Przybylek, and Caroline Fitzgerald, who have embraced partnership with us with open arms to bring whiskey history programming to life over the past five years. And double thanks to Leslie Przybylek, who graciously stepped down from her curatorial perch at the Heinz to offer a beautiful foreword to this humble book.

Many thanks also to Eric Meyer, who spent six months putting together the tour about the Whiskey Rebellion that we still use today at the distillery, and that helped frame the outline for the Whiskey Rebellion chapter. His brother, Jeffrey Meyer, our family librarian and archeologist, spent countless days pouring over contemporaneous materials in the rooms of the Carnegie Library.

The comprehensive books by Thomas Slaughter and William Hogeland were invaluable in understanding the events that comprised the Whiskey Rebellion and their context. We recommend these works to anyone who wants to dive deep into this topic. An anonymous author put together an Overholt family history which we relied on heavily. Martha Frick Symington Sanger's biography of Henry Clay Frick is one of the most beautiful and haunting biographies and reading it was one of joys of writing this book. We also highly recommend Quentin Skrabec's Frick biography, which was of great use in our research.

On the craft spirits front, we owe thanks to Michael Kinstlick, who did much work to capture the early growth of craft distilling, and to Harry Kohlman, who is always one of the smartest people in the room—no matter the room. Harry has given more thought than likely anyone to the future of craft distilling, and kindly suffered through many conversations on the topic with us.

Thank you to Anne Trubek, who came to Pittsburgh and convinced us to bring this nascent book to life. She has been an amazing support and is a visionary force in developing and growing regional identity throughout the Midwest and Midatlantic. We owe a deep thanks as well to Anne's team: Michael Jauchen, who patiently and thoughtfully edited this text, and to Nicole Boose who cleaned it up again thereafter. Thank you also to Meredith Pangrace, John Tarasi, and Jessica Pierson Turner who each lent their design talents to this process.

We were lucky to have some of the region's most talented bartenders: Drew Cranisky, Angela Smalley, Cecil Usher, and

Dawn Young, take time to develop cocktail recipes for this book. The other cocktails included here draw heavily on the work of Wes Shonk from his time on the Wigle team.

Without customers at the distillery, we wouldn't have had the opportunity or the platform to tell this regional history and so we thank everyone who has visited us in Pittsburgh!

And finally, we give special thanks to Mary Ellen Meyer and Alexander Grelli who kept constantly feeding us tidbits and edits while offering endless moral and childcare support. And to Effie, who put up with many summer Saturdays filled with far too many binders and books and too few hours at the playground—thank you. We love you all so much.